Absolutely Amazing Ways to Save Money on Everything

JAMES L. PARIS

HARVEST HOUSE PUBLISHERS
Eugene, Oregon 97402

Cover by Left Coast Design, Portland, Oregon

**ABSOLUTELY AMAZING WAYS TO SAVE
MONEY ON EVERYTHING**

Copyright ©1999 by James L. Paris

Published by Harvest House Publishers
Eugene, Oregon 97402

Library of Congress Cataloging-in-Publication Data

Paris, James L., 1965–
    Absolutely amazing ways to save money on everything / James L. Paris
      p. cm.
    ISBN 1-56507-917-5
    1. Finance, Personal—Religious aspects—Christianity. 2. Saving and
    investment. 3. Consumer credit. I. Title.
HG179.P226 1999
332.024—dc21   98-42238
                                                      CIP

Printed in the United States of America.

99 00 01 02 03 04 05 / BP / 10 9 8 7 6 5 4 3 2 1

To Terry Paris and the other men who modeled Christ during my childhood.

My Uncle Terry Paris, who has recently recovered from cancer, has been a great inspiration in my life. For years he took me to a Christian boys club on the south side of Chicago while I was growing up. He was my little league coach and raised six kids—putting most of them through college on an electrician's salary. I am the product of what he and many other men did to help a young boy learn about life.

Also, thanks and appreciation to my father James L. Paris, Sr., my next door neighbor Joe Coniglio, my Uncles Johnny Atherton and Everett Hines, my Grandfathers Carmen Paris and George Atherton, my other little league coach Jack Payton, my former pastors Dave Scott and Phil Nelson, and Bob Good, my high school band director.

Thank you for giving to the Lord; I am a life that was saved.

Acknowledgments

I wish to thank Bob Yetman, my researcher and writing assistant, for his countless hours in compiling this book. As always, without his efforts this book could not have been written. I also wish to thank Ray Duhon, Karen Tibbets, and Patricia Castro for their assistance.

Contents

Making Your Money Count 7

1. Eating and Dining Out for Less 9

2. Looking Good on a Budget 25

3. Save Money on Health Care 43

4. The Best Deals on Furniture and Appliances . . . 61

5. Saving Money on Home and Yard
   Maintenance 79

6. Transportation Savings 97

7. Investment Strategies 123

8. Lowering Higher Education Costs 143

9. Reduce Legal Expenses 159

10. Great Trips; Great Prices 197

11. Big Savings Online 217

Appendix A: Factory Outlet Malls 229

Appendix B: No Commission,
Direct-Purchase Stocks 235

Appendix C: No-Load Mutual Funds 245

Bibliography 249

Making Your Money Count

As Christians, we are called to honor God with our finances. I believe that how people handle their money truly impacts their entire lives. Our checkbooks and calendars tell us more about ourselves than almost anything else. Where we spend our time and our money are two of the greatest factors in our lives. Some people say that money is evil and any book, seminar, or program about making or saving money is consequently bad as well. This is not a biblical view or philosophy that is borne out by any historical truth. Some of the most influential people in the Bible were wealthy—David, Solomon, Abraham, and Job just to name a few. Everything we do can be done to bring glory to God, including how we manage our finances.

The issue is not how much money a person has, but rather how he or she manages it. It seems to me that there are at least two major ways to approach any financial transaction. In general, most people take the easiest route when it comes to spending money. Since businesses in America know this about our character, they take full advantage of it. For example, how much easier can it be to buy a car than walking into the dealership with no money down and driving out in a new car in about an hour (not to mention the five-year payment book you get as well). It would be much more difficult to look through the newspaper and find a two- to three-year-old vehicle, have it checked out by a mechanic, and arrange your own financing. Yes, this takes time and energy—but it saves a lot of your money! In a typical auto purchase, you may save well over $10,000 in price and interest by investing this extra time. In your lifetime, you will probably buy four or five cars.

This means you may save more than $50,000 over the course of your life.

This book encourages you to go the extra step—a move I believe to be well worth your time. If you choose to adopt the everyday, common-sense strategies contained in this book, you too will be able to stretch your dollar farther than ever before. What it comes down to for most is that getting their finances in order is as simple as either making more or spending less. This book is not about spending less and getting less, but living the *same* lifestyle you are living now for less money by being a smarter consumer.

For you and your family, I wish you the best of success in your pursuit to make the most of the money that God blesses you with.

1

Eating and Dining Out for Less

I realized the value of food when I went off to college. The Christian college that I attended provided six days of meals and closed the cafeteria on Sundays. Sundays were days of hunger for many of us in those times, but we had a tried and true strategy to get by. We would skip breakfast and wait until about two o'clock to eat at a local "all you can eat buffet." This strategy allowed us to make it on just one meal for the day. I think I remember the cost being about four dollars; I guarantee that they never made money on me or my friends at The Duff's in Springfield, Missouri.

Have you ever stopped and wondered just how much money you and your family spend on food and eating out? Just for fun, write down all of the food-related expenses you incur during the course of a week to see how you make out. Statistics show that we spend anywhere from 10 to 20 percent of our incomes on food and eating each year. With those kinds of expenditures, it only stands to reason that there is some room available to lower costs and realize savings.

Let's face it: Eating is one of the few simple pleasures that we all get to enjoy. Sure, we eat to live, but most of us also enjoy eating, as well. So in this chapter you won't find ludicrous suggestions like eat nothing but plain, white rice every night of the week or limit your nights out at restaurants to scrounging around the dumpsters looking for scraps. No, I've written down several sensible strategies you and your family members can use to keep the amount of money you spend on food down to a minimum without drastically altering your eating habits.

Government statistics show that the typical American family has the capability of cutting its food expenses in half without having to sacrifice nutrition or the enjoyment that comes with eating the things we like so much. Now, I should tell you up front that you will not find suggestions in here on how to eat healthier. This is a book about saving money, not about living longer. However, I am all in favor of people eating good, healthy food and you should know that resolving to eat healthier can be, by itself, one of the easiest ways to cut expenses. Fresh fruits and vegetables can make marvelous and less expensive substitutes for pricier processed foods that are not terribly good for you. Consider this your first strategy to saving money on food . . . eat right!

Grocery Store Principles

 Make a list . . . and stick to it!

You may have heard this before, but having heard it before in no way diminishes its correctness. Before you depart on your weekly shopping trip, make sure you have your list in hand. Detailed research has yielded the following information: The average shopper purchases at least one item per aisle that he or she had not otherwise intended to buy. Note that it was one extra item *per aisle*, not just per trip. At that rate, it's easy to see how a weekly trip to the grocery store can end up costing a lot more than it needs to. By using your list, you have given yourself a better measuring stick against which you may exact your self-discipline. Now, of course, there's nothing that says you must strictly adhere to this list. However, most of us will refer to the list and keep close to its parameters when we enter the supermarket.

Even with a grocery list in hand, many of us are successful in rationalizing why we need this or that item—items that were not on our list to begin with. Only you can ultimately decide to pick up, or refrain from picking up, that additional item and placing it in your shopping cart. One excellent strategy I use whenever I head for the grocery store and find something unexpected that I just "have" to have involves making a point of stopping to write that item on my list . . . and then putting a mark next to it. While I try not to make a habit of picking up unplanned items at all, I have my moments, and I like to see how much my lack of discipline in the store ended up costing me. The next time I go, then, my inclination to adhere to the list is usually much stronger.

The list method can be very effective. I know of one person who sticks to his grocery list without any variance. He and his wife sit down before the weekly grocery trip and carefully make out their list. They take the time to go from one end of the house to the other and identify those things they will need that week and write them down. If they get to the store and realize they forgot something, they do not buy it—even if it is something important. These two have adopted the philosophy that if they had their wits about them and took the appropriate amount of time when they did their planning, they should not forget a thing, and their punishment is to go without for that week if they do happen to forget. That strategy may seem a bit extreme, but it is an approach that has served them in good stead financially through the years.

*Pay close attention
to the unit price of an item.*

If you spend much time examining the packaging or shelf information of a food product, you will notice that there are generally two prices listed: the regular product price and something called the *unit* price. Understandably, the vast majority of us pay attention to only the product price. Not only is it the most prominently displayed of the two prices, but it is also the price we will actually pay at the checkout counter for the product we have in our hands. However, the truth is that the unit price, not the product price, may well be the price to which we should be paying greater attention.

The unit price shows you how much you are really paying for something on a "pound-for-pound" basis. It also tells you how much something really costs. For example, you may pay a lower product price for a package of 6 XYZ hotdogs, but on a unit-cost basis, you'd pay less if you were to buy the larger-sized package of 8 ABC hotdogs. The total product price might be higher with ABC, but your real cost would be less because you would be receiving more for your money.

The benefit of unit pricing, then, is that it allows the shopper to determine if it is better to buy a given product in bulk.

Save a bundle when buying meat.

It is said that roughly one-third of our money spent during a trip to the grocery store is spent on meat and poultry. Obviously, this won't apply if you're a vegetarian, but for the rest of us, it generally holds quite true. There are some strategies you can implement when you go shopping for meat that have the potential for substantially reducing your overall food bill.

Frequently people make the mistake of reaching for the meat package they're seeking that has the lowest price. Don't be pulled into that trap. *Bottom line:* When it comes to buying meat, shop the cut, not the price. Poor quality cuts contain a lot more fat, gristle, bone, and so on. The pricier cuts will be much leaner, giving you more for your money and, thus, better overall value.

If you insist on buying a cheaper cut of meat, here's an idea you can employ to make that piece of beef more palatable. By marinating tough cuts of meat for extended periods of time, you will tenderize it and be able to enjoy it more fully. It works just fine and the meat tastes great. This is an easy way to put more money in your pocket when shopping for meats.

Grocery Coupon Strategies

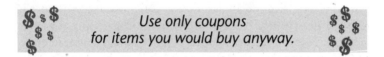

*Use only coupons
for items you would buy anyway.*

How many times have you perused the coupon books contained as a supplement in your newspaper and caught yourself thinking, "Hmm . . . *that* looks good. . . . I can use this coupon to buy it cheaply now." Well, if what caught your eye was a product you don't normally purchase, then guess what? You're about to add to your food bill, not subtract from it. I remember running across a friend of mine at a clothing store where everything was on sale. When I asked her what she was doing (knowing full well she was shopping), she replied with an impish grin, "I'm saving money!" We both laughed out loud at the ridiculousness of the logic and went about our respective ways.

Well, the same logic is used by shoppers in grocery stores all over the country every single day of the week. People see a coupon and decide they're going to "save" money by buying the item when it's on sale. In reality, they wouldn't have bought the product at all if they hadn't seen the coupon.

Coupons provide a wonderful way to save money at the grocery store, but first and foremost, you must resolve not to buy anything you wouldn't normally buy.

Accumulate coupons.

The trend now in grocery retail is for food manufacturers to shy away from using coupons in favor of more permanent "lower" prices. Nevertheless, there are still copious numbers of coupons available for grocery store use, and this will likely continue to be true as long as research indicates that many shoppers can be coupon-driven. An excellent strategy involves paying more attention to your coupon potential, in this case by accumulating as many coupons as you can for the goods you normally purchase. One thing you need to pay close attention to is the expiration date on the coupon, but many coupons have expiration dates for as long as a year, so there is ample opportunity to save using them. Developing a large cache of coupons can really come in handy when you need to buy nonperishables because you can buy them with your coupons and have no fear that they will go bad before you have a chance to use them.

Trade coupons you don't normally use for those you do.

Another excellent way to maximize your coupon potential is to trade the coupons you don't use for those you will use. Grocery store coupon booklets are filled with coupons for all sorts of items that you simply don't use, whether it's because there's no need for the product within your family, the brand name is not a favorite of yours, or you just don't care to buy what's being offered. That's quite understandable, but why are you throwing out those coupons you don't use? How come you're not taking advantage of those coupons by trading them? That's right, trading them. It is quite likely that there are many people who will have a use for the coupons you don't want. For example, maybe you don't have babies, but a friend does. Why not offer to trade coupons you come across for baby food and other baby products in exchange for coupons you can use for your family?

There are very creative people out there who have set up all sorts of coupon-trading clubs and forums. Find one of these coupon clubs—or better still, set up one of your own. Establish a network of other grocery shoppers (friends and relatives are a great place to start), and begin a practice of clipping and trading coupons. By doing this you will maximize your coupon savings more than you ever thought possible.

 Use your coupons to purchase the smallest size possible.

Bigger is not always better, and nowhere is that more apparent than in ventures to the grocery store (not that it's *never* better, just that it's *not always* better). Case in point: Whenever you decide to use a coupon, it's usually a much better deal to use it on the smallest size of the item available to you. Many coupons from food manufacturers are designed so that they can be used on an array of sizes of the given product. Cereal is a good example of this. Cereals come in a variety of sizes, and when coupons are issued from cereal companies, they're often good for at least two or three of the available sizes of the particular cereal. Coupons are not issued on a percentage basis; that is, it's one coupon for one flat price's worth of savings, so you might as well use it on the smallest size, the one that typically has the lowest price. As a result, you're out-the-door cost will be as low as it could possibly get.

 Save your coupons to use during sales.

One of the biggest wastes of coupons is to use them much too quickly. Usually a coupon-clipper uses the coupons they accumulate the same week they come to possess them. My advice? Don't be in such a hurry! There will be several opportunities during the year when the products you have come to know and love will be placed on sale. Get in the habit of saving those coupons and using them when the sales are on—thereby increasing your savings even more. There are even some important timing guidelines to which you can refer with respect to when to use coupons, most significantly this one: Sales on couponed items generally take place about a month or so after the coupons are published, so keep your eyes peeled for the sales.

The savings you reap can be amazing. It is not all that unusual to find individuals who are able to pay not much more than a few cents for a food product, and there are those who can sometimes actually get an item free!

 Increase your coupon-buying power on the web.

The modern age can be a beautiful thing. While there are many reasons why some of us may look with chagrin at what modern times have brought us, there have clearly been some innovations that make our lives easier, as well. One of the recent innovations in this regard has been the advent of the mass-produced personal computer, and its companion tool, the Internet. Using his computer, a person can access the Internet and its countless numbers of resources through which an array of services may be performed and products purchased. On that note, I'd like to present to you one of the newest and neatest resources for Internet-accessed grocery shoppers: Coupons on the Web!

There are a number of coupon websites you may review and download coupons for use on behalf of a variety of goods and services, most notably grocery purchases. A few of the-on-line coupon sources include Coupon Connection (www.couponconnect.com), CouponMail Online (Connecticut) (www.couponmail.com), and E Clip (www.eclip.com), but you can review a laundry list of coupon websites by accessing the James L. Paris Companies webpage at www.jlparis.com, and then searching for "coupons."

Bring your lunch from home.

Another simple strategy which many of us discard without seriously thinking through how much it costs is what we spend on lunch when we leave the workplace to eat out. Let's assume that you can buy lunch each day for $5 (knowing all too well that the sum can easily reach $10 or more, depending on the restaurant selected). That $5 per day translates into $1,300 per year. Now, let's say that you buy lunch food from the grocery store each week with the intention of making your lunch at home and bringing it with you to work each day. How much would that cost? Well, a recent trip to the grocery store for one of my staff yielded a week's worth of lunch foods that averaged just under $2 per day. That's a savings of $780 per year! And you can eat just as heartily—and even healthier—by creating your own lunches at home.

I realize that "brown-bagging" lunch may not be a preferred choice for you, especially if you are a professional, but make no mistake about it: There is a lot of money to be saved by playing it smart and bringing your own lunches from home. Besides, when you finally sit atop the corporate ladder and no longer feel obligated to be so careful with money, perhaps you'll be able to thank, in part, this strategy for the fact that when you were working your way to the top, you still had money in your pocket at the end of each month.

Stop kidding yourself . . .
and buy generic brands.

Most of you know you have the option of buying generic alternatives to the well-known brand-names of many products sold in a grocery store. Do you buy generic brands? Do you know that many generic brands available are actually manufactured by the same companies that make the well-known brands? Well, it's true. (Well, it's not true in *every* case, but it is true most of the time.) Get in the habit of purchasing the generic, or supermarket, brand of foods and products when you go to the grocery store. The savings can vary, but it can be more than 50 percent.

As I said, well-known companies manufacture many, but not all, generic brands. Some generic brands offer great savings, but may not have the taste you've come to expect. So experiment. Try the generic brand of each type of food product you buy at the store when you run out of it at home. Eventually you will know which products you're satisfied about purchasing generic, and which items you'd rather purchase by name brand.

 Center your food purchases around budgeted meals.

Budgeting is a word many of us do our best to avoid because it connotes work, discipline, deprivation . . . and might be associated with a host of often-unpleasant thoughts and tasks. However, if you really want to save money at the grocery store, shop for budgeted meals. Clearly plan your meals for the week *before* you sit down to make your grocery list. Choose meals that fit into your overall budget for household expenses.

This is a strategy more about the wisdom of household budgeting than anything else. After all, before you can plan each meal, you need to know how much money is available for food purchases. I'm not going to go into a detailed discussion of budgeting here, but if you want to learn how to set up a household budget and stick to it, you may want to refer to my book *More for Your Money* (published by Harvest House and available at your local Christian bookstore).

Once your food budget is established (the monthly/ weekly allotment of the family's financial resources available to spend on food), you may now move on to the task of budgeting your meals. Give yourself the amount of money you have to spend each week on meals, and take it from there (remember not to use all of your grocery funds on budgeted meals; there will be other items you'll need to buy that will not be directly related to meals). If you've never done this sort of thing before, it may take some getting used to. However, the savings realized at the grocery store is worth the effort. There is nothing like heading to the supermarket with a well-planned, strategically designed grocery list that helps you save money—sometimes in spite of yourself!

Saving Money When You're Eating Out

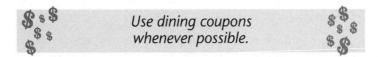

Use dining coupons whenever possible.

Certainly the idea of taking advantage of a coupon offer at a local restaurant can hardly be called unbelievable, but what *is* rather notable is how prevalent restaurant coupons are. In fact, it's possible to get a hold of so many that it may be very difficult to use them all in a reasonable span of time, but then that's the great thing—you can have plenty to last you for a long time. The best way to develop a solid supply of dining coupons is to purchase the coupon books in your area that are published by Entertainment Publications or other organizations. Entertainment Publications specializes in publishing coupon books that pertain to all general areas of leisure activities, such as dining, lodging, and entertainment. What's more, although many of these coupons are set up to provide flat percentage-rate discounts from total meal prices, some offer great deals like the "two-meals-for-the-price-of-one." That's how you *really* end up saving.

If there's an unfortunate aspect to coupon opportunities like these, it's that they are under-utilized. I can remember buying worthwhile coupon books for $5 and $10 from kids selling them door-to-door to raise money for school ventures, only to take the books and throw them into a kitchen junk drawer, never to be used and eventually to expire. What a waste. Such coupon books often sport hundreds of dollars of values. The dining coupons published by Entertainment Publications can cost as much as $50, but they offer the opportunity to save a small fortune over the course of your dining-out existence. Take it from me: They are one of the smartest investments you'll ever make, but you have to actually use them for the investment to pay off.

 Skip dessert and pocket substantial savings.

One of the most enticing aspects to eating outside of the home is the opportunity to partake of the wonderful creations made in the restaurant bakery. I must confess that *I* am sometimes very tempted to order dessert when dining out when the plethora of sweet concoctions available lets my normally parsimonious nature be guided by my heart (or would that be tastebuds?) as opposed to my head.

Nevertheless, I normally opt out when the dessert menu is presented, even when the giant sampler tray of what's available (how cruel can you get?) is brought to the table. I'm not saying that I never order dessert when I'm out at a restaurant, but the instances when I do are pretty rare. The reason? Well, besides the fact that my waistline doesn't need any help in its expansion efforts, I am aware of the fact that desserts in most restaurants have the highest mark-up. Small dishes of ice cream, which cost little more than 20 or 30 cents at the wholesale per-serving level, command prices of well over a dollar in restaurants, which means that your dealing with a mark-up over five times above cost.

Dessert is a good part of the meal to pass on at the restaurant and wait to eat it at home. Not only will you be keeping yourself from ordering the priciest (relatively speaking) items on the menu (and saving yourself anywhere from 10 to 30 percent, by most estimates), but you are also not diminishing the quality of the restaurant dining venture for you or your companions because dessert is the last course of any meal experience. By passing on dessert, you're just choosing to leave a little early.

Select franchises for the best value in outside dining.

Private or independent restaurants are those that usually carry with them the best reputations as far as food quality goes. In elevated social circles, franchises are considered to be quite boorish, and while the food quality at independents can oftentimes be superior to that found in franchise or "chain" establishments, the best value in general still rides with the franchises.

In fact, it is value that is considered the hallmark of most franchises. There are many franchises that offer a lot more than fast-food opportunities, and some are even quite good. I am personally aware of an Italian chef who eats at a well-known Italian franchise restaurant quite often because she feels it represents the best combination of food quality and value.

Experts believe you can save as much as 30 to 35 percent by choosing a franchise restaurant over an independent for the same meal. This value is often realized most fully when kids are present at the restaurant because many franchises offer tremendous deals for kids' meals, even including opportunities from time to time when children can dine for free.

Create a full meal for yourself from the appetizer, soup, and salad menus.

One of the biggest problems with eating out is that oftentimes you receive more than you can really eat. This is great if you brought a huge appetite with you or if you are content to take the unfinished portion of the meal back to the house so you can eat it later. But the truth is that you will have still paid a pretty penny for your food.

If you want to realize solid savings at a restaurant—and get enough to eat without facing the prospect of stuffing yourself—why not avoid the entrée section of the menu altogether? If you peruse the appetizer section of the menu, as well as the soup and salad section, you should be able to come up with a variety of different meal combinations that will more than satisfy your palate, while giving you the opportunity to save money in the process. Have you ever seen some of those baked potatoes that are in vogue now? They look as big as small footballs when they come to the table, and with all of the trimmings they're usually topped with, they can be as filling as any entrée. By following this strategy, you can easily save yourself 50 percent off the cost of a "regular" meal.

Cookware Shopping Tips

 Buy your cookware at the K-Marts and Wal-Marts of the world.

Cookware boutiques are very popular these days. It's rare to enter a mall in America these days and not stumble across a specialty shop dedicated to the sale of chic cookware items of all shapes, sizes, and purposes. However, the problem with these kinds of establishments is that while they may seem like the places to shop out of deference to their specialization, the fact is you will be paying way too much for what you're getting.

The same is true of cookware purchased at upscale department stores. For some reason, it seems as though doing one's cookware shopping at these kinds of establishments is the most appropriate route to take, but that notion likely rests on little else besides a throne of pretentiousness. You should be able to satisfy almost all of your cookware shopping needs very nicely at your friendly, local K-Mart, Wal-Mart, or another discount department store similar in style. Granted, it's not likely that you'll be able to find the same kinds of upscale cooking supplies at Target that you'll be able to find at one of the fancy specialty stores, but how much difference does that make?

The key to the savings lies in the fact that these stores are able to buy in volume, whereas the smaller establishments can't buy in bulk money-saving quantities. Additionally, these discounters cater to their cost-conscious customers who wouldn't even think of paying high prices for common household items. It is not at all unusual to realize tremendous savings buying your cookware at discount stores—as high as 75 percent in some cases. (I'm not saying that you'll save 75 percent on the same piece of fancy cutlery, for example, that you would find in an upscale shop. What I am saying, however, is that you can realize that kind of savings when purchasing an item that has the same purpose, usability, and lifespan as the same item that is a lot pricier, perhaps solely out of deference to its more aesthetically pleasing appearance.)

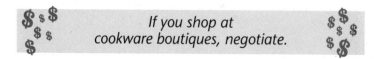

If you shop at cookware boutiques, negotiate.

One of the best-kept secrets in the world of cookware shopping is that it is as acceptable to negotiate the price of the items in the same way you can bargain on the price of a new car. The inside scoop in the cookware biz is that a consumer should seldom pay full price for his choices. Cookware retailers will definitely accept less than the price listed, and there is actually more opportunity to save when it comes to the really expensive items. The cookware industry is such that retailers all have essentially the exact same products, so you should have a lot of bargaining power—if you choose to use it.

2

Looking Good
on a Budget

I have worked with a number of individuals over the years on creating budgets. My initial assignment is for them to put together a list of all their family expenses. Although most people forget to list clothing in their budgets, they don't show up naked for their appointment! Clothes are an expense that can really impact the pocketbook. But there are, thankfully, a lot of opportunities for Americans to save when it comes to clothes shopping. The reason for that is clothes have some of the highest mark-ups on the retail side of any type of product available. It is not uncommon for the mark-up on clothes to be as high as 500 percent over wholesale, and the truth is that it can be much higher. Shoe prices in particular can be some of the worst offenders, which is one of the reasons why so many discount footwear retailers make a killing selling nothing but shoes.

Currently, Americans are spending well in excess of $100 billion per year buying clothes at malls and department stores—that's *billion*, with a *b*. That's more than $500 per year spent for every man, woman, and child in the country. What's more, that figure doesn't take into account the copious amount of money spent in the off-mainstream clothing retailers like outlet malls, mail-order houses, and Internet stores. Just a cursory review of these figures should tell you that it's quite possible to reduce your clothing costs substantially. In this chapter you'll find simple yet effective strategies that will help you save money.

 Remember the two best times of the year to buy clothes.

Summer clothes bought during the summer season can be had for a sizable discount. One might hear that and say, "Well, of *course* summer clothes will become cheaper once summer has started . . . that's true for any season." To an extent that's correct, but there's still bigger savings in summer. The reason? Besides the savings factor associated with purchasing seasonal clothes well into the season, summer also offers an advantage because of what normally transpires during the season itself. The long, hot days of summer normally make a higher percentage of the population a bit lazier than they might otherwise be, and thus these folks will be less likely to head to malls when they have free time. Additionally, summer usually means vacation time for a lot of families, and as a result sales drop in malls and department stores during the summer months, thereby clearing the way for bargains.

In addition to summer, there's another time of the year during which clothes-shoppers should be prepared to reap great rewards—the weeks following Christmas. The month of January is, overall, a terrific time to enjoy great savings on clothes purchases. Retailers usually stock up heavily before Christmas, and do not generally intend to restock before the spring inventory arrives at the end of January and beginning of February. The savings on clothes purchased in the month of

January can be as great or even greater than 50 percent off the retail price of the garments.

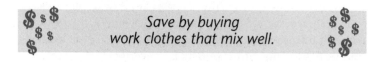

*Save by buying
work clothes that mix well.*

A lot of people who work in an office environment that is at least semiprofessional believe they need to dress to the hilt in expensive suits. Well, whether you are male or female, assembling several professional business suits for use at work can cost you several hundreds to thousands of dollars. But you can assemble a wonderful array of professional business attire far more cheaply than you think.

Men: Rather than purchasing that pricey two- or three-piece suit, why not get some different combinations of sports jackets and slacks that will go well in a variety of combinations? This can be an especially worthwhile strategy if you work in an office environment where you aren't expected to wear your jacket all day long. Oh, you may need to have at least one truly nice suit for very special occasions, but for the rest of the time why sweat it? Additionally, if you carefully select nice varieties of shirts and ties, elements that can help bring your whole ensemble together, you should still be able to look like a million bucks. By purchasing neutral-colored jackets and slacks, you'll usually be able to find the style you're seeking without going broke in the process.

Women: Purchasing "separates" can be the key to dressing stylishly without breaking the bank. Blazers, skirts, and slacks are the three key separates that you should buy in order to dress far more cheaply than you would if you purchased a couple of expensive suits at a local boutique. You need to have at least one formal business suit in the closet that can be worn on truly special occasions, but otherwise, "mix and match" your way to dressing for success.

*Women, buy men's clothes
when appropriate.*

Here are some strategies that my wife, Ann, has con-
tributed to save money on women's clothing. These may take
traditionalists and other purists by surprise, but there's one
undeniable fact in the world of clothes-shopping: As with hair-
cuts, women pay a lot more for their clothes than do men. In
many cases, the price differential for essentially similar items is
around 50 percent, and it can easily be more. Now, ask yourself this question: Except for the obviously female-unique
kinds of garments like skirts, dresses, and bathing suits, is it
really necessary to do all of your shopping in the women's sections of department stores? Lots of casual clothes, like T-shirts,
collared polo-style shirts, blazers, and even dress shirts are
gender-interchangeable. The savings realized can be especially
pronounced when it comes to athletic wear. Working out is all
the rage these days, and if you are a participant in these sorts
of activities, you know that much of the athletic wear made
available to women is extremely "high-end." Save yourself a
small fortune and buy men's workout apparel at every opportunity.

You may feel a little silly at first looking for clothes for
yourself in the men's departments, but don't. It is quite
common for women to wear men's clothes, and as long as the
sizes are appropriate, determining the gender for which they
were originally made will be well nigh impossible.

*Learn to distinguish genuine
outlet stores from the pretenders.*

In these days of increased consumerism and greater overall
cost-consciousness, the outlet store has gained great favor with
the consuming public at large. However, to really benefit from

outlet shopping, there are a few things you need to know. The first thing is how to identify an honest-to-goodness outlet store.

Just because a store refers to itself as an outlet, or takes up residence in an outlet mall, doesn't necessarily mean it is a *real* outlet store. Legitimate outlet stores are those where manufacturers sell their own merchandise directly to the public. These stores are quite singular in that a particular store will sell only the merchandise from the manufacturer whose name is on the sign out front. For example, the established men's clothier Van Heusen has an outlet store here in Florida. The store sells only Van Heusen clothes, which makes it a true outlet. However, many of the "outlet" stores found in outlet malls are really "liquidators." Liquidators differ from outlets in some important ways, including brands sold and merchandise quality. Liquidators generally specialize in providing a home for merchandise that is discontinued, slightly damaged, and so on—items not regarded as very desirable, which means that you may not be very happy with their selection, even if the name on the label is that of a well-known manufacturer.

 Shop for irregulars. They may be a better deal than you think.

Lots of you out there are going to be really particular about this, but I'm telling you: If you want to save a bunch of money off the full-retail price of something, get used to the idea of buying "irregulars." Irregulars are garments that have some minor flaws, not significant enough to prevent their sale, but flawed, nonetheless. As a result, they are sold at a discount. The biggest laugh I get out of irregulars is that nearly every irregular garment I've ever run across looks perfect to me. The only way to determine that a garment is truly irregular is to scan it very closely, and even then the flaws are not always identifiable. The beauty for the shopper, however, is that manufacturers will sell these garments at prices well-below retail as an alternative to throwing them out altogether.

Instead of thinking "I would *never* wear an irregular," consider the money saved. Irregulars present the opportunity for significant savings, and you're able to purchase, for all intents and purposes, the same item of clothing for which you would otherwise pay full retail prices.

 Dig into the sale barrels, boxes, and bins.

Very often when you enter a department store (and especially an outlet store), you will find large racks, barrels, boxes, and other types of bins filled with clothing that the store is trying to close out once and for all. The reason this clothing is discounted can range from that which has simply proven to be unpopular, to returns, to irregulars. Therefore, you need to be careful as you make your selections to ensure that the items you select have the level of quality you desire. This can be especially important when the store maintains a policy that "all sales are final," which they frequently do with merchandise sold in this fashion. Nevertheless, the hassles can be worth the effort, as the savings on merchandise like this can be 50 percent or more off retail.

 Save big at department stores by obtaining a store credit card.

If you know anything about my philosophy with regard to the use of credit cards in general, and department store credit cards in particular, you're probably quite surprised to read that I would recommend that you go out and sign up for one. As you may know, department store credit cards represent some of the lousiest deals in credit cards overall. Not only is their use limited to just that store itself, but the interest rates charged are among the highest in the credit-granting industry. So why would anyone suggest that you obtain one of these little "bank account destroyers" in an effort to *save* money?

Well, the answer is not so difficult to understand. Anyone who has ever held one of these cards knows that cardholders often receive special sale opportunities, including access to "private" sales where the store is open for a limited period of time on a given day only to cardholders, employees, and so on. Your store credit card, then, is not to be used as an actual purchasing mechanism, but rather as a tool you can use to access better sales opportunities in your stores of choice. But remember to maintain the discipline required to keep from using these cards; keep them for their strategic usefulness and nothing more.

 Bargain for retail clothes purchases.

Have you ever wondered why it's considered so acceptable to negotiate the prices on cars, large appliances, and other types of goods so typically sold retail, and yet when it comes to clothes, which actually have some of the highest profit margins in mainstream commerce, you almost never hear of it being done? Well, you *can* bargain down the prices in clothing stores, under the right circumstances. It's just that no one ever seems to think to try.

The best opportunities to try and negotiate down the listed prices of clothes come when you're looking at clothes that are already being sold at a discount. If it's on sale, what does that tell you? That it's not selling, or at least hasn't sold thus far. Stores are eager to rid themselves of this merchandise as quickly as possible because they have new inventory arriving all the time. If you are smart and a little tough, it shouldn't be difficult for you to enhance your savings on already-discounted merchandise even further.

What should you look for? The best thing to look for is a garment you like that is on sale—and one that you can see a flaw of some kind on. I'm not necessarily talking about an irregular; in fact, getting a discount on an irregular is not likely because the store already knows about the garment's flawed nature and likely took that into account when they priced it. No, what you want to find is something that is priced to sell quickly but also has a small flaw of some kind not yet noticed by the store. If you find something like that (and they're not tough to find on sales racks, given how many hands have touched, pulled, and tried on the garments by that time), approach the clerk and make an offer that is roughly 15 percent under the listed price. If you offer too little, then the answer will certainly be "no" because even at that level the assumption that "someone out there will definitely pay this price" will kick in. So be smart regarding your offer and do it in a way that will assure the highest possible degree of success.

One note of caution: You'll hardly ever be able to negotiate down the prices on merchandise being sold at regular rates. These are usually clothes that are doing well for the store, which means that if you don't buy it at the listed price, it probably won't be long before someone else does.

Formal Wear

Over the course of your life, you will attend special occasions from time to time that may require you to wear something formal. Formal wear is often regarded as the most expensive type of clothing available, and with good reason; nevertheless, it's not necessary to go broke attiring yourself for the occasions that demand you step out looking regal.

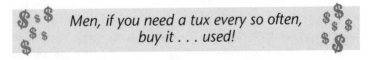

Men, if you need a tux every so often, buy it . . . used!

I don't care where you go to rent a tuxedo . . . after you have paid for all of the various accouterments that go with the actual tux itself—including shirt, shoes, tie, and cummerbund—you will be hard-pressed to be out the door for less than $100 for one rental. Now, ask yourself how often you will need a tuxedo. If it's more than three times, you may want to buy that tuxedo and be done with the rental stores once and for all.

"Hey, a tuxedo would be great, especially one for which I don't have to be constantly fitted, but those things are expensive," you say. Not necessarily. Tuxedos are unique in that most people who own them wear them very infrequently, so that if you seek to buy one, buying it used will not be a move that will mean you are sacrificing appearance in order to save money. In fact, there's no reason you can't purchase a used tuxedo that will make you look every bit as good as a new one. Take your time, shop a lot of different places, and then make your selection. You may be surprised at how far your dollars will take you. If you're not convinced, just do the math: You should be able to buy a quality used tux (with all of the extras that go with it, except for shoes) for about $150 or less. This means that you're already saving money once you've worn it twice, and then the savings just become greater each time after that.

 Women, opposite strategy—rent your formal wear.

Wouldn't you know it? What's good for men when it comes to saving money on clothing is not good for women. It goes back to the sometimes-strange disparity in prices between men's clothes and women's clothes. In the case of formal wear, women are usually going to be better off renting that drop-dead gown than they are buying it. It's all a matter of price.

As I mentioned above, men can buy a sharp-looking, second-hand tuxedo for not much more than a $100. Women, alas, don't have that option. Most designer gowns will cost well over $1,000, and it's hardly uncommon to pay upwards of $2,000. Amazing, isn't it? Well, if you're expecting to use a gown like this just a few times in your life, why not rent instead? Renting an upscale gown can be done for roughly $150 to $250 a shot; pricey for a rental, to be sure, but even if you have an occasion to wear such a gown seven or eight times in your lifetime, you'll likely come out ahead by renting instead of buying.

In fact, there are more and more people who are choosing to rent their wedding gowns as opposed to buying them. I realize that to some this choice almost seems sacrilege, but think about it seriously for a moment. Do you realize the number of people who spend fortunes on wedding gowns, only to never lay eyes on them again once they are packaged for long-term storage? Unless you really feel that there is a substantial likelihood the dress will be used once again, renting it is really not a bad idea at all. Or, if renting is just too distasteful an idea, shop at one of the growing numbers of "bridal warehouses" that seem to be popping up all over the place these days. As the consuming world becomes increasingly cost-conscious, there continues to be entrepreneurs willing to take advantage of that sentiment by making goods and services available at discount outlets. Bridal gowns and bridesmaid dresses are absolutely no different in that regard. The cost of weddings is legend, and, until recently, no one spent much effort trying to consider if weddings were even an appropriate place to cut costs. Well, life's realities are such nowadays that most people have little shame when it comes to these sorts of things. And, many level-headed folks on limited budgets realize they can vastly improve the overall quality of the wedding and the reception experience by spending much less on gowns and dresses, and more for food and other items that will make the experience more memorable and enjoyable for everyone.

 When ordering by mail, be sure to use a debit card.

Shopping by mail is extremely convenient, and it's possible to reap quite a savings. Mail order houses don't have the overhead that regular department stores have, so it's not unusual to enjoy a measure of savings as a result. True, there isn't ever going to be much of a chance for you to buy the irregulars or heavily discounted merchandise that we've spoken about previously, but by using mail order, there's ample opportunity to save on regular clothing you would find in major department stores. However, one of the major downfalls to purchasing clothes via mail order is that you are generally limited to transacting your purchases with credit cards. Even if you have the money readily available to purchase your items, the payment options are limited to using your plastic or sending a check. However, as times have changed, there is now a way to enjoy the convenience of credit cards without enduring the associated expenses, especially the high interest rates.

Very popular now is something called the debit, or check, card. The debit card is a Visa card that doesn't access a line of credit but draws the amount of your purchases straight from your checking account. The debit card is a feature of checking accounts offered by banks. So many banks offer them now, that those that don't are clearly the exception rather than the rule. The beauty of the debit card should be readily apparent: It allows you the opportunity to make your purchases with the Visa card, but taps the money in your checking account. This means you can pay for your purchases up-front with no running balances, interest rates, or annual fees to face. You can, of course, use the debit card anyplace Visa is accepted.

Now, be forewarned that because of how these cards work: *You are paying as you go.* There is no balance being built up with your purchases that may be paid at a later date. The money is coming *straight out of your checking account when you make the purchase.* The debit card's advantages strongly outweigh its disadvantages, and comparing debit cards with credit cards is really like mixing apples and oranges. *They are two different financial tools.*

If you don't possess a debit card currently, contact your bank to see if you can obtain one. If your bank doesn't make them available, you may want to consider moving your account to one that does. Debit cards are that useful and convenient.

> *When ordering by mail, ask questions before making the purchase.*

Convenience is clearly the chief advantage to ordering by mail. It really is the only reason for doing it. After all, if you're one who enjoys the typical shopping experience, you're hardly going to enjoy it by sitting at home and thumbing through a catalog. Some catalogs do offer garments that are tough to find elsewhere, but for the most part, convenience is the bottom-line reason for shopping in this fashion. However, the line between *convenience* and great *inconvenience* with respect to mail order shopping is very thin. Anyone who has had to return something ordered through the mail will knows what I mean. The hassle of repackaging something that didn't fit or was otherwise unsuitable, together with the bite associated with paying the return postage, can turn a mail-order shopping experience into something most unpleasant in a heartbeat.

Does this mean you should forget about purchasing garments via mail order? Not at all, but it does mean you need to be extra vigilant to ensure you've limited, as much as possible, the chance that your order will need to be returned. The best way to do this is to ask questions. In fact, you should ask a lot of them, covering concerns related to size, fabric care, shrinkage, and a host of other matters that will directly affect the usefulness of the garment to you. The funny thing is, most people ask these questions to themselves but fall mute when they call to place the order over the phone—or don't call at all if they're mailing in their order. Save yourself a huge headache and write down any questions you have so that you'll be prepared when you call. That way you'll receive the answers that will help you make an informed decision before you place your order.

If you change your mind about a purchase after you've placed an order, you can always refuse to accept delivery. While following that tactic probably won't win you any friends at the mail-order house, it is a bottom-line way to avoid going through the efforts necessary to return goods you know you don't want.

 Purchase your garments secondhand.

Secondhand. Hand-me-downs. There seems to be an array of terms available to describe previously worn clothes that are still useful. Usually, we think only in terms of exchanging clothes intra-family, but the fact remains that you can put a lot of money back into your pocket. If you're smart about it, you can dress every bit as well as someone purchasing new clothes. Being smart about it means learning the best places to shop in your area and being willing to put some time into your efforts. I know many people have a built-in aversion to wearing used garments. Clothes are personal enough that it makes it difficult sometimes to feel comfortable wearing those worn by a total stranger. However, if you can get past that, there's *a lot* of money to be saved. Clothes available second-hand usually cost only a small percentage of the full retail price at which they were sold when they were new. Remember, if you can save on clothes, it can be your most substantial savings on consumer items, overall.

 To buy the highest-quality used clothing, head for the consignment shops.

Oftentimes the terms *thrift* and *consignment* are used interchangeably by people who are describing second-hand clothing stores, but make no mistake about it—the two are not the same. Let's take a quick look at the differences so you have a better idea of what you can expect from each.

Thrift stores are not-for-profit establishments that are usually run by charitable organizations. The clothing available at these locations is donated, for the most part, which means the selection may not be that terrific. Heading to the thrift store is probably not a good choice for someone who wants to save money while still dressing somewhat stylishly.

Consignment shops are different. First of all, consignment shops are private businesses that are trying to make a profit. The clothes sold through a consignment shop are donated, but when they are sold the donor receives a portion of the revenue as a commission, if you will. Primarily, consignment shops sell women's wear, which is probably just as well considering how much women are normally forced to pay at the regular retail level.

The bottom line is that although you may be in the market for used clothing, the consignment shop route is going to be far superior to thrift stores. The savings may not be quite as substantial over thrift shops, but they will clearly be significant over retail. If you're willing to work at it, you may find that your local consignment shop is a veritable gold mine.

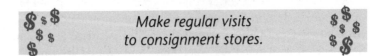

*Make regular visits
to consignment stores.*

What in the world does that mean? you wonder. As we've just discussed, second-hand stores present some of the best opportunities to save money. One effective strategy you can use to save even more is to make a habit of going into the store on a regular basis, whether you intend to buy something that day or not. By making yourself a "regular," you can strike up a good relationship with the clerks and the manager. What's the reason for that? Well, with used clothing, there can be lots of room for negotiation and deals. By becoming well known as a good customer in a consignment or thrift store, you will likely enjoy a more favorable response should you try to get a better price on a garment than that which is listed. Also, if you are on the lookout for something in particular, you can feel more comfortable about making a special request to have something held for you.

The After-Purchase Care of Your Clothes

One of the best ways to hold down the expenses associated with overall clothing costs is to make sure you are maintaining and caring for your garments in a way that causes the least amount of wear and tear on them. If you make a point of taking as good and as gentle care of your clothes as possible, you'll find that you'll need to buy a lot fewer of them during the course of your lifetime.

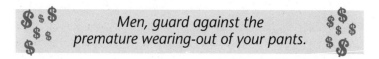

Men, guard against the premature wearing-out of your pants.

In general, a man's pants are the first thing to go in his wardrobe. Be they casual or formal, it is, specifically, the so-called "seat" of a pair of men's pants that will wear out over time. Most men resign themselves to this occurrence and simply expect to spend the necessary funds to replace the pants. But by following a few simple steps, you can vastly improve the longevity of your pants, and keep your clothing costs down to a minimum. I know personally of one person who hasn't bought a new pair of pants in over ten years by following these steps . . . and he always looks like a million bucks, too!

When it comes to dress pants for which you must be fitted, ask the tailor to line them. Lining is very inexpensive, usually under $10, but it can make all the difference in whether you have to go out in a year or two to purchase another pair of pants. Also, with respect to dress pants, you may want to buy a second pair of them when you're buying them as part of a suit. The extra pair of pants won't significantly add to the cost of your suit, but will significantly decrease the likelihood that you'll have to replace the suit because the pants are worn.

As for more casual pants, you can save wear and tear by using the patches that you can find in fabric stores, convenience stores, and grocery stores. The crotch is the part of the pants that wears out so frequently for men. By investing in some replacement patches, you can vastly extend the life of your pants. The key is to not wait until you've worn a hole in them, and then patch them; rather, patch them first, at the point where you know from previous experience the holes will eventually turn up. This simple strategy will work on all fabrics, including denim, and will add years to the life of your pants.

 Use stain removers before giving up on any clothing item.

When was the last time you went looking for stain remover? There are a lot of excellent stain removers available on the market these days that do a masterful job of removing the messes that life's little complications can sometimes leave behind. There's probably a special section in your grocery store aisle dedicated to these little wonders. You may have to try a few to see which work best for you. Also, you may find that using two or more in combination with one another will yield the best results.

Most of us are probably unwilling to take the time to apply stain remover, wait for it to settle in, and then wash our clothes, but that's a mistake. The stains that our clothes pick up are among the biggest reasons why we end up discarding them eventually. This can be especially true of perspiration stains. However, there's no reason to endure these messes and resign yourself to tossing out your expensive clothes because of them. The very best way to ensure the longest stain-free life for your clothes is to apply the stain remover as soon as you see a problem and let it sit for a while. By taking this small step of clothing care, you can easily find yourself spending a much longer amount of time *in* them.

Keep enough clothes in your closet.

Perhaps the first rule of properly caring for your clothes is to see to it that you don't have to wear them too often. If you are wearing "favorite" clothes all of the time, you will clearly have problems keeping them well maintained for very long. Although it may seem a "wash" (pardon the pun) as to whether you wear a few clothes more often and then replace them, or spend the money at the outset by purchasing several different outfits, the truth is that you will be able to keep all of your clothes much longer if you have enough of each to keep from having to wear any of them out.

3

Save Money
on Health Care

I have had many experiences with health care and hospitals, many more than I would have liked. I had many a trip in an ambulance—before my tenth birthday! There's a saying, "Anyone who thinks that money is everything has never been sick." Truer words have never been spoken. Pain or ill-health of any kind, no matter how minor, has the unfortunate ability to significantly diminish the quality of life for all who are afflicted. Adding insult to injury (pun intended), though, is the fact that the cost of treating illness is high, and getting higher all the time. Even if you are one of the very few people in our society who has managed to exist just fine without having to face any kind of substantial medical problem, you are probably keenly aware of the high cost of health care from the news agencies which seem to have something to report about the subject almost nightly.

Estimates suggest that health-care costs currently rise at the rate of 10 percent per year, and there is no sign of that rate slowing. What's more, it's not simply the direct costs of health care that rise, but also the associated expenses. Take health insurance—same problem. It stands to reason that if the cost of getting well is going up, then the costs of insuring one for those costs will also rise.

Unfortunately, even though there's lots of inflation within the health care industry, there is not a lot of room to do the kinds of cost-cutting that we can do in the other consumer areas of our lives. If you want, you can fire your pool cleaning service and do the work yourself; however, can you take out your own appendix? You can't do that even if you *are* a doctor. Also, there are no "slow seasons" in medicine. People of all walks of life, afflicted with all kinds of physical problems, are getting sick everywhere and everyday in our world. The medical community by no means needs to offer discounts or coupons to generate business.

Does this mean there are no opportunities to save money in this area? Not at all. It *does* mean, though, that you will have to look a little harder and work more diligently in this area to realize savings than you would have to in other areas. What follows in this chapter are strategies you can use to save money in several different facets of medical and health care. Read each strategy carefully, and try to incorporate it as fully as possible into your daily life. Whether direct medical costs, pharmaceutical costs, or health insurance costs are your biggest worry, this chapter should be able to assist you in dramatically reducing your expenses. In fact, I've taken the liberty of including a roster of common ailments in this chapter, as well as some treatments you can do yourself. Now, without further delay, let's find some absolutely unbelievable ways to save money in the area of health care.

Saving Money at the Hospital

While health-care costs seem to be out of control everywhere, they are downright obscene with respect to the area of hospital costs. Have you had the chance to examine an itemized hospital bill lately? Yikes! No wonder some people actually get worse after an extended hospital stay. Perhaps the most egregious price gouges are in the areas that should be (you would think) among the very cheapest . . . like the cost of pillows, tissues, and so on. It is not unusual for a substantial, inpatient medical procedure of some sort to cost tens of thousands of dollars—and costs in the hundreds of thousands are not at all rare.

What you need to do is learn now how to save money in the event that you find yourself facing a hospital stay of some length. Yes, it's true that if you have health insurance (which you should always have, no matter what; we'll talk more about that a little later) you will likely have a substantial portion of the costs covered. However, many policies require deductibles and copayment provisions that mean you may have to personally help to absorb the burden, which can mean spending thousands and thousands of dollars. Can your budget stand that? Can anyone's?

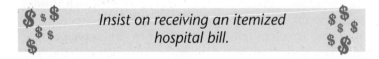

Insist on receiving an itemized hospital bill.

Okay, I mentioned hospitals, so let's lead off with a sharp strategy *regarding* hospital bills: Insist on receiving an itemized bill at the end of your hospital stay. Few hospitals will automatically make an itemized bill available, but they will do so if you make a special request. Make that request. Numerous studies have shown that the vast majority of hospital bills contain errors. In fact, you may be shocked to learn that "vast majority" in this case means over 90 percent. Ninety percent! This means that you have more than a 9 in 10 chance of being handed an incorrect hospital bill when you leave. What's more, these same studies have shown that almost always the errors in these bills work to the advantage of the hospital and to the distinct *disadvantage* of the patient.

When you receive your itemized bill, be sure to take the time to go over it carefully. It does no good to demand the bill and then glance over it quickly. If you have questions, don't be shy about asking them. You know the deal—if you won't stick up for yourself, who will? Remember, too, that even if an insurer is paying for your bill, you should still hold the hospital accountable for any overcharges or other errors you find. After all, it is these kinds of problems that are making health insurance the cash cow it seems to be for so many providers. Do us all a favor and check your bill carefully.

 Have your procedure done on an outpatient basis.

Modern medicine has made it possible for many treatments that used to require an inpatient stay to be done on an outpatient basis. Either that, or different, less invasive and traumatic treatments have been substituted that allow for much shorter, less physically impacting trips to the hospital.

There are a lot of procedures that can be conducted on an outpatient basis that previously had no alternative to the costlier, more involved treatments of the past. I realize that the increased use of outpatient procedures to help cure traumas and ailments are good for the insurance companies, and some of you now will not like them solely out of deference to that reason. But it's quite possible to get efficient, quality same-day service on ailments as significant as childbirth and hernia operations, to name two. When your doctor presents you with the specter of having to go the hospital to have an important, but by no means life-threatening operation, quickly ask if you can go on an outpatient basis. Find out if what's ailing you has a quicker treatment that doesn't require you to spend more than a few hours at the hospital. If it can't be done, then at least you asked . . . but push for it to be done.

When you check in, make sure you're turning down unnecessary items or things you can provide yourself.

Hospitals are big business; if you want to know how big business they are, wait and see what your itemized bill looks like when you finally checkout. Do you realize that when you partake of a hospital's in-patient services, you are signing up to be charged a ton of money for things that normally cost very little? One of the reasons for this is that when you have, say a need for a tissue, you are charged not for the number of individual tissues used, but rather you are charged for the cost of the whole box that was opened just for you.

The best way to get around this is to tell the hospital that you don't want to be charged any more than necessary, and that you'll check to see if you were charged for the whole box of so-and-so, as opposed to being charged for them on an individual basis. Be prepared, as well, to bring the things you'll need from home. Family and friends can easily bring you tissues and such. Also, be advised that pillows, gowns, and slippers will leave your wallet begging for mercy if you allow the hospital to provide them for you. Hospitals will nickel and dime you on everything, but when it comes to these sorts of items, it is hardly nickels and dimes that will be exiting your piggy bank. Believe it or not, we're usually talking hundreds of dollars per day that you're paying just for these basic needs.

To get around paying a not-so-small fortune for personal items like robes, arrange with the hospital's billing office *before* you go in to have yourself set up so that all concerned, especially the hospital, will know that you will be bringing in these items from home. Do not wait to take care of this once you get there to check in; contact the billing department beforehand so this can be worked out well in advance to avoid the chance of errors. Additionally, be sure to get the name of the person in that department with whom you spoke, so that you have some added insurance should something go awry and you find yourself being handed these things, anyway.

 Do not allow yourself to be subjected to tests without an excellent reason.

This is sort of a continuation of the previous strategy. At county hospitals that are pretty much required to take in and care for anyone, regardless of their capacity to pay, all staff members pay close attention to ensure that routine but expensive tests are not done on a patient without very good reason. However, if you have insurance (and remember, even if you do, you are probably subject to a copay provision of some sort) or simply a better capacity to pay for the bills, it's quite possible that your doctor(s) will not be nearly as thrifty regarding these routine and sometimes extremely costly tests that can quickly add thousands of dollars to your overall hospital bill.

Before you agree to any "routine" test, find out from the doctor why it is necessary. Now I realize that it may be tough for you to tell from what you're told if a test is really necessary or not. But if you sit right up and ask the doctor to explain, you will be taking a proactive role in your treatment, letting the doctor know that you want to be involved. Listen carefully to what he or she says. If the procedure makes sense, then go with it. If, however, the doctor doesn't sound convincing, you may want to say "thanks, but no thanks." It is, after all, your money, as well as your health.

 Have your meals brought to you from home.

Meals are another part of the hospital bill that can cost you a bundle. Hospitals retain special dieticians to formulate menus, and this kind of specialization costs. Although hospital food is not nearly as bad as it used to be, it seems like you'll be paying for that improvement—and paying a lot. Sidestep all of that by having your family and friends deliver your meals to you from home. As long as your in-hospital diet is not required to be too specialized, you should have no problem being granted permission to have this done.

I realize that by the time you've prearranged to have your tissues, robes, slippers, and meals brought to you from home and you've chosen to be an active participant with your physician regarding the tests you may be scheduled for, you may gain a reputation at the hospital as a tough customer. It will be worth it, however. By sticking to your ideas, you can literally save thousands of dollars on your next trip to the hospital.

 Save yourself a fortune by shopping around for hospital services.

Shopping around, regardless of what it is you're seeking, is still one of the best, albeit most underused, money-saving strategies in existence. You can really save on some goods and services by shopping around. Auto insurance, for example, is downright famous within financial planning circles as an area wherein a consumer can save huge sums of money simply by calling around for rate quotes. The cost differences for the same coverages can vary by as much as 70 to 80 percent from carrier to carrier. Well, as it turns out, shopping around for hospitals can possibly help you realize the same levels of significant savings, too.

Numerous studies have shown that for essentially the same services, hospitals can vary in price by as much as 100 percent. Fortunately, most physicians maintain affiliations with at least two hospitals, which means that in a worst case scenario, you will have the opportunity to take advantage of some degree of choice. If you're worried that maybe the hospitals will not want to spend the time to give you the quotes you're seeking, don't be. My experience has been that hospitals are usually pretty good about providing estimates to prospective patients before they walk through the door for their stay. As with any good strategy, it only works if you're willing to use it, so don't be shy. Get an estimate!

Doctors

Sooner or later, nearly all of us will require the services of a doctor. Those services rarely come cheaply, and while none of us would normally think of our health or the health of our loved ones as a place to do much penny-pinching, it *is* possible to obtain quality medical services from a doctor without paying a fortune. To do this, however, you need to be aware of simple strategies that you can implement in order to make the savings a reality.

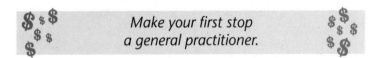

*Make your first stop
a general practitioner.*

General practitioners (GP), also known as "primary care physicians," are usually regarded as the "first line" of doctors. In fact, most group insurance providers will not pay for you to see a specialist unless you've been to a GP first. Now why do you suppose that is? Because specialists charge a lot of money for their services, and in truth, they may be worth every penny . . . as long as you really need their services. However, general practitioners are adept at handling the vast majority of maladies with which you may become afflicted. How much will you save if you opt for the GP? It can be as much as 50 percent. That's a sizable percentage, especially when you're talking about doctor bills.

Please don't misunderstand me. Specialists are by no means doctors to be avoided if you have a serious or unusual condition. But going to see an ear, nose, and throat specialist for a sore throat is usually a complete waste of money.

Negotiate with a doctor over his or her fee.

Have you ever heard the expression "everything's negotiable"? Well, surprise, you can even negotiate with a doctor over his fee—or at least you can try. The point is, it's not at all unusual to see a doctor reduce his rates if you have the ability to pay cash for your services. Many physicians abhor the hassle that processing insurance claims and making collection efforts put their offices through. Even if you have health insurance you might consider this option. If you don't need to go to the doctor very often, there's a good chance that you won't even satisfy your deductible requirements. If you have a $500 deductible, for example, it may take several office visits (even at today's rates) for you to meet the deductible, at which point you begin to receive reimbursements for your expenses.

So rather than working toward your deductible bit by bit, paying full price in the process, why not strike a bargain with your physician? Tell him that if he's willing to discount your bill substantially, you'll pay him right then and there for his services...no insurance claims to process, no administration, no nothing. If you want, you can call the doctor's office before you arrive to see if this strategy is even possible to use in your case. As far as your insurance goes, worry about using that when something more substantial than regular check-ups befalls you.

If you're in an HMO, get your medical help over the telephone.

The way an HMO, or health maintenance organization, works is that the doctor will receive a certain amount of money per patient. Whether the doctor sees you 100 times or not at all, he will receive the same sum of money. As a result, it is not difficult to have your doctor help you with valuable advice, even money-saving advice, over the telephone.

Now, it's not likely that if you have not yet been to the doctor about a new condition you have, he will be able to do much for you over the telephone. He will probably want you to come in so that he can make a basic evaluation, even if what you have is quite common. This strategy is most useful in circumstances where you're dealing with follow-up appointments. In other words, perhaps you're due for a follow-up appointment to see if you need to continue with a particular treatment. Well, if your condition wasn't bad to begin with, then it may be possible to determine from the phone call if you really need to continue your treatment. There are a lot of scenarios that could arise where accessing information from your doctor over the phone is quite prudent. For individuals covered in plans like HMOs, the phone is an excellent resource to reduce unnecessary hassle and expense.

 Unless you're in dire straits, don't go to the emergency room.

Many people are inclined to go to the emergency room even if they don't have a genuine emergency. Going this route may seem like a simple, straightforward answer for some, especially for people who don't go to doctors very often, but it is hardly a bargain. It is nothing for a visit to the emergency room to cost twice what an office visit costs, and beyond that, there's no guarantee that you would see someone faster than if you had your own physician and arranged for an office visit.

For example, let's say that you awakened in the morning with what you suspect is bronchitis, or perhaps pneumonia. If you have a regular doctor and call him that morning, there's an excellent chance that he or she may be able to fit you in at some point that day, perhaps even that morning. Your trip to the emergency room, though, is potluck. You may arrive there at 7 A.M. and not be seen by a doctor for several hours. Plus, people with genuine emergencies are usually seen first, regardless of arrival order. That will push your waiting time back further still. Finally, after you've been seen, you will find that your emergency room visit will cost you way more than your office visit would have.

What should you do? If you don't have a regular doctor, get one. This allows you the freedom of choice. It also makes getting in to see a doctor a lot easier. Too many people don't think about obtaining a regular doctor until after they've had a bad emergency room experience. And even then, they sometimes never bother with finding a personal physician. You can handle your medical needs like that if you want, but you can save a lot by planning ahead and being prepared.

Insurance

Health insurance represents for many of us the key to realizing the services we need to stay healthy during the course of our lives. The problem with health insurance, however, is that as the costs of health care go, so go the costs of health insurance. (The United States is one of a very few number of developed nations that doesn't have national health insurance. The reasons for this are complicated, and cut sharply up and down the full range of the political spectrum. Our discussion is not about politics or the pros and cons of national insurance, however. Rather, I want to help you make the most of what is available to you.)

There are ways to save significant sums of money on the cost of health insurance, but you may find it interesting that the first strategy I'm going to present to you is one that actually asks you to spend money . . . because, by spending money, you stand to keep a lot more of it in your pocket in the long run.

*Maintain some form of
health insurance.*

What is insurance? In a nutshell, it's a mechanism whereby you pay small sums of money to insure yourself against a much greater potential financial loss. Just on the basis of that simplistic definition, you should be able to see why you should never try to save money by doing without valuable types of insurance coverage. Health insurance is, along with auto, homeowners, and life, an essential type of insurance for you to maintain.

It is no secret that the biggest problem with quality health insurance is affordability. If you are not a member of a group health policy, it is oftentimes cost-prohibitive to purchase that kind of comprehensive coverage on your own. So what can you do, then, when there is no affordable access to full-coverage health insurance? Simply go without any kind of health insurance?

The short answer to that question is no, but let me explain. I have found that too many people see health insurance as a comprehensive coverage that allows for $5 prescriptions, $15 office visits, and so on. That is the wrong way to look at health insurance. Health insurance should be viewed as a means to ensure that your family doesn't fall into bankruptcy as the result of a family member suffering a serious illness or injury. The $5 prescriptions are nice, but having to pay full-price for medicine and doctor visits won't devastate your family financially. What will is the financial loss that results when you try to pay the medical bills associated with a catastrophic medical illness or injury. The reason you need to maintain coverage isn't about day-to-day medical needs; rather, it's about insuring against disaster. To do that, all you need is a relatively inexpensive major medical policy.

Major medical insurance policies, also known as "hospitalization," will cover your bills in the event of a medical catastrophe. Major medical is health insurance without perks or "bells and whistles." It exists solely to cover the major expenses so that you will not be financially ruined in the event of severe injury or illness.

Major medical policies will vary in price from carrier to carrier, but they will always be substantially less than the cost of comprehensive, group-type coverage. You should be able to look in the Yellow Pages of your phone book in order to shop around for a low-cost major medical policy. When you do, here are a couple of things to keep in mind.

First, maintain as high a deductible as you can. (The deductible is the amount of money *you* must pay for medical services.) The higher the deductible, the cheaper the premiums will be. If you want to reduce the cost of coverage further still, look into the copay (copayment) provisions that are a common part of these plans. With copays, you are essentially committing to pay a percentage of the bill, up to a certain dollar amount (after which point the insurer pays the whole thing). A common major medical copay is 80 percent/20 percent, up to $5,000. This means that in the event of a loss, you will be on the hook for the deductible, as well as 20 percent of the first $5,000 (after the deductible is paid). Once the bill tops the $5,000 mark, the insurer pays the rest.

As you can see, major medical insurance is not particularly glamorous, but it is functional and can mean the difference between financial death and survival in the event your family suffers a substantial medical loss.

So you see, insurance is a great example of how spending money may save you a fortune in the future. True, you may never need it, but are you willing to take that chance?

 Look for a group you can join to obtain group medical coverage.

We just spent a few minutes talking about health insurance in general and major medical in particular. We know we should have at least major medical in order to ward off financial woes should calamity strike. This does not mean, however, that you should give up looking for group coverage. Group health insurance is clearly the best deal, offering the most perks for the lowest coverage. However, the reason it's available to groups is because it is the groups who, with their money pooled, can afford to pay the substantial premiums. It is possible to gain access to a group policy even if you aren't working at a regular job. Group means group—there's no stipulation that the group must be one of workers. There are group policies, for example, that cover members of clubs, credit unions, and organizations. You may have to do some digging, but it should be possible for you to find a group in which you can participate.

Saving Money on Pharmaceuticals

Clearly one of the most expensive aspects of health care for individuals and families is the cost of drugs. Increases in drug prices have been astronomical over the past several years—roughly three times the rate of inflation! A very frustrating aspect of this for consumers is that pharmaceutical companies, in general, are making a tremendous amount of money, much more than most other large corporations. While we can digest the information and spend our time being angry at these entities who admittedly appear, at times, to be conscienceless profiteers of the sick and elderly, it would probably be more useful to pick up a couple of strategies we can use to vastly reduce the costs for medicine.

 Go for generic alternatives when you need drugs.

When you need medicine, your doctor will often prescribe a well-known "name" drug. You might think that's what you would want, after all, who wouldn't want top-of-the-line medicines when sick? The problem is that these well-known, brand-name pharmaceuticals are very expensive. They're so costly because the companies that manufacture them must make back all of the money they put into research, production, and sales. And they need to make a profit. But it would be foolhardy to ignore the possibility that part of the problem is that, at some point, some people in the industry decided to take advantage of those who need medicines to get well.

Is there a way to get around these high costs? You bet there is and if you're not using it, you're throwing your money away. What I'm speaking of is using generic alternatives. Generic drugs are, on average, about half the cost of brand-name drugs, and yet are essentially the very same medications. I say *essentially* because the generics may use fillers that are lower-cost alternatives to those used in the name brands. But fillers really make no difference since it's the active ingredient(s) that matter.

When you're in your doctor's office and he or she is preparing to prescribe something, always ask if there is a generic alternative available. If there is (there isn't always one available), ask for the generic. If the prescription has already been written, ask the pharmacist about a generic alternative when you get it filled. If he can oblige you, he gladly will.

 If you need a lot of medicine, consider ordering by mail.

If you have a condition that demands you effectively stay on medication of one type or another, you may want to look into mail-order pharmacies. Your doctor should be able to give you a list of mail-order services that will fill prescriptions long-distance and send them to you. The benefit to receiving your medicine this way is that mail-order houses typically offer very cheap prices for those who order in large quantities. If you can do that, you may save as much as 50 percent off the cost of your prescriptions . . . and that is not chump change.

But don't automatically assume you'll save by ordering through the mail. Get a price quote first. Only then will you be able to decide if mail-ordering your medicines will indeed offer significant savings.

Self-Help Medical Treatments

You've undoubtedly heard the expression, "Physician, heal thyself!" Well, here, the expression could more accurately be, "Consumer, heal thyself!" While I am a big believer in wasting no time to get to a doctor or to a hospital in the event you seem to have something significantly wrong with you, it is possible to save money by using home health remedies that are well-known within the medical community, but may not be as well-known to you.

Now here's the caveat that you've likely been expecting: Under no circumstances should any of these remedies be regarded as a substitute for professional medical care. Furthermore, I am not a medical doctor. I am choosing to make available effective, self-help treatments through this book, but responsibility for your own well-being must lie with yourself.

Acne (not severe): Reduce the level of oiliness on your skin by wiping it with astringent witch hazel or astringent pads like those put out by Stridex. The best over-the-counter treatment for mild acne is benzoyl peroxide, and it can be found in various concentrations in a variety of products. Steam is also effective against acne, specifically for unclogging pores. Boil 2 cups of water with ¼ cup of either the herb chamomile or fennel. Reduce heat and simmer. Place your face over the rising steam. After 10 minutes, rinse your face with cold water.

Athlete's foot: Soak affected feet in a mixture of salt and warm water (usually two teaspoons per pint). Mitigates perspiration and fungus growth.

Insect stings and bites: Apply a paste made from meat tenderizer containing papain, and water. This mixture will break down the protein-based venom.

Burns (**minor**): Apply ice to the affected area, take aspirin or ibuprofen to relieve pain and inflammation, and apply aloe vera gel (a substance proven to accelerate the healing of burns) to the wound. (It's a good idea to keep an aloe vera plant in the house for just this purpose.) Apply the aloe vera after the heat in the wound has substantially subsided.

Bronchitis: Drink a lot of fluids to liquefy bronchial secretions, and use a humidifier or vaporizer to add moisture to the air. Try not to suppress coughing because it brings the phlegm out of your lungs.

Constipation: Drink a lot of fluids, which will help soften the stool. Beverages containing caffeine have been shown to help with constipation. Mineral oil can be effective, as well. If none of these approaches works, try an over-the-counter laxative (stool softener). Enemas may be used, but not regularly. If the problem continues or occurs often, contact your doctor.

Corns: Walking on sand will do the trick with corns. The sand helps "sand" away the corns.

Diaper rash: Warm cornstarch in a thin layer in a baking pan to about 150 degrees. Let the cornstarch cool then spread over the baby's bottom.

Diarrhea: Consume Gatorade (or other rehydration fluids). Begin a diet known by the acronym BRAT (bananas, rice, applesauce, and toast). Do not do this with an infant. People with hypertension need to carefully monitor the high level of sodium in some of the "athletic" drinks.

Foot odor: Prepare a mixture of tea and water (two tea bags to a pint of water), boiling the tea in the water. Add about two quarts of cool water. Soak your feet from 5 to 30 minutes.

Headaches: Apply ice packs to the forehead, cold, wet towels to the neck. Massage head, neck, and shoulders. Try using pressure points at two areas: press thumbs into the "hollows" on either side of the neck (at the base of the skull) then press on the fleshy area where the thumb and forefinger come together at the back of the head. Press and relieve pressure in increments of approximately 30 seconds. Take one of the following: aspirin, ibuprofen, or acetaminophen. Those afflicted with chronic migraines may decrease headache occurrences by chewing the herb feverfew or by ingesting it in capsule form. Be advised this is not a quick fix, but a remedy that may take a couple of weeks to produce results.

Hemorrhoids: Apply petroleum jelly to the affected area. (Petroleum jelly is really the active ingredient found in many over-the-counter hemorrhoid medications.)

Muscle Strains: Treat with R.I.C.E. (an acronym for rest, ice, compression, and elevation). After about a day, substitute heat for ice in an effort to increase circulation. Also take aspirin or ibuprofen to reduce pain and inflammation.

Poison ivy: Apply a paste of baking soda and water. Or you can apply gauze soaked in cold milk, which will dry the poison ivy and provide itch relief.

Stuffy nose: Eat spicy foods that contain ingredients, such as hot pepper and Tabasco, that burn the mouth. (Or chew the spices directly.) Sniffing an onion can also be effective.

4

The Best Deals on
Furniture and Appliances

While your home may represent your single biggest investment, sometimes it seems like the things you put *into* your home are really your biggest cost items. Furniture and appliances can easily run into the tens of thousands of dollars, depending on the home and the people who live there. If you don't believe me, stop and think for a moment of all you have in your house by way of furniture and appliances (go ahead and include consumer electronics such as appliances, for the sake of this discussion). Start from one end of the house and go to the other; consider everything. Now, could the sum total spent on all of that reach the $10,000 mark? Absolutely.

Outfitting our homes with the kinds of furniture and appliances that make our at-home lives comfortable, easier, and more enjoyable *can* cost a fortune—but it doesn't *have* to!

You probably know that the most common way to save money on both furniture and appliances involves buying these items used. My experience has been that buying used furniture and appliances can represent some of the greatest shopping values. Many people are content to let go of beautiful, functional appliances and furniture for ridiculously low prices because they need to move out of their homes with urgency, raise cash quickly, or many other reasons that are common to our existence.

By the end of this chapter, you should never again have to go to the poorhouse, even temporarily, to ensure that your home has the kinds of creature comforts we all love to have to enhance the enjoyment of our homes.

There are many things you can do to decrease your furniture expenditures now and in the future. First, I'm going to show you how to save money buying new furniture, then we'll talk about how to save a bundle by buying used—and still get quality in the process.

 Negotiate for the furniture you want.

Perhaps the best, most straightforward way to save money on new furniture is to haggle over the price. Furniture retailers are no different than so many other kinds of retailers in that they clearly give the impression that prices on furniture are nonnegotiable. It's not true. Expensive furniture, which we all know can run well into the thousands for a single piece, is just as viable an opportunity for negotiation as your car, house, or other goods that are more traditionally thought of as being the kinds of items conducive to negotiation. Essentially, whenever you are buying any kind of item for which the salesperson is compensated by a commission, you have room to move—especially when you're talking about very "high-end" items where the mark-up can be formidable.

A couple of tips: First, if you can, pay cash for the furniture. Cash *always* speaks louder than any kind of credit arrangement and, as a result, presents more of an opportunity for you to negotiate some money off your deal. Also, you may want to do some comparison shopping. If you find another store carrying the same merchandise for a more competitive price than the one you started in, go back to the first one with the price information from the second one in hand. Because of the tremendous competition between furniture retailers, you may be able to get the first retailer to not only match the offer of the first, but beat it by 5 to 10 percent. In fact, if you want to try and negotiate a hard bargain, don't just hold out for a matching offer; after all, if that's the best he can do, you have no motivation to buy from him over the one that priced the furniture lower to begin with. However, point out that you're standing in his store *now*, and you would be happy to do a deal if he can undercut the competitor by an amount you think is reasonable, like the aforementioned 5 to 10 percent.

Finally, you should know that most furniture retailers are not willing to offer less than 10 to 15 percent off of the standard prices of their pieces. I say this because I don't want you to think you can drive a really hard bargain and walk away with a steal. Remember, you are always competing with all the consumers out there who blindly walk into a store and pay full-price for something without batting an eye. If you offer too little, the salesperson will say no in a heartbeat because he or she knows the chances of someone else coming in to buy the piece at full-price are very good. Nevertheless, when you're standing there ready to buy, a salesperson may be willing to throw in a bit of a discount to get the deal done.

 Take advantage of the latest trend: Borrowing for free.

They seem to be all over the place these days—those deals that allow you to buy expensive goods on credit with outrageous terms that favor the consumer. You can buy appliances, carpet, all kinds of things that way—and usually leading the pack in these kinds of opportunities are furniture retailers.

Do you know of what I'm speaking? I'm talking about those credit deals that offer 90 days, 180 days . . . even one year "same as cash" on your purchases. What better way to buy something expensive like furniture than to give yourself a year to pay for it—for free? Typically the programs work like this: You purchase your furniture with the stipulation that it's delivered now, but you won't be obligated to begin making payments on it until some point in the future. With these same-as-cash offers, if you are able to completely pay off your purchase during the same-as-cash period, you will owe no interest.

Can you imagine buying $5,000 worth of furniture, having it delivered immediately, and still having a year to pay for it without facing interest charges? You can easily save yourself hundreds, even thousands of dollars this way. You can thank America's monstrous consumer debt problem for these kinds of opportunities. Faced with the realization that so many consumers are "maxed out" both in terms of monthly budgets and existing credit lines, retailers have had to find creative ways to move their inventory and still make a few bucks.

Be forewarned, however. All same-as-cash deals are *not* created equally. The biggest difference has to do with accruals. With many of these deals, even though you're not required to begin making interest payments until the prearranged designated point in the future, the interest you *would* owe accrues on your bill from day one. This is an important point. If you do not pay off your principal balance by the end of the same-as-cash term, you will be on the hook for *all* of the interest that has accrued to that point and will continue to accrue if you delay paying off your purchase in full. If you still owe even a dollar on your principle balance when the same-as-cash period clicks off, all of the accrued interest comes due.

The issue of accruals on these deals is important because if you miss paying off your principal balance in full by the cut-off date, your deal is significantly weakened. For best value, keep your eye out for same-as-cash offers that not only delay payments for the period, but delay accruals as well. This would mean that if you paid nothing at all toward your balance for the entire period, that at the point your same-as-cash window closes, your interest charges would start accruing then. It is, by far, the best deal of these already-great deals.

One more thing. It behooves you, no matter how your specific same-as-cash deal works, to get the balance paid off by the appointed time. The interest charged by furniture retailers is typically around 21 percent, and it's not negotiable. In other words, it doesn't matter how pristine your credit history is—you'll get whacked for these exorbitant interest charges if you don't pay off the balance on time.

 Order your furniture from the manufacturer.

In general, whenever you can cut the middleman out of something, you save money. When it comes to buying furniture, you can save a lot. North Carolina is regarded as the furniture capital of the U.S., with roughly 400 manufacturers based around two principal areas within the state. If you want to save big, go to the source which, in this case, means North Carolina.

Furniture manufacturers in North Carolina are renowned for making their inventory available through huge outlets. What's more, because so many people travel to North Carolina to buy furniture in this fashion, there are many hotels located near these outlets so you don't need to go through a lot of hassle to make your furniture-buying trip. Hearty souls throughout the country rent the size truck they think they'll need from U-Haul or Ryder and drive to North Carolina to buy and take their new furniture home. If you're thinking, "Well, this sounds good, but I'm sure that I would lose whatever savings I would earn through the cost of the trip." Don't bet on it. Not only is it common to buy furniture this way for as much as 75 percent off the retail price, but you avoid paying the sales tax you'd be charged in your home state. Now, don't get me wrong; this isn't the thing to do if you're in the market simply for a coffee table. But if you're looking to outfit at least one key room in the house with top-of-the-line furniture, then a trip to North Carolina may be well-worth your time and energy. That's why it's important to figure out the cost of the furniture and the trip ahead of time. Of course, the *more* you're looking to buy . . . the greater the savings.

Alternatively, if you're not interested in traveling to North Carolina to buy furniture, but want to try to take advantage of the savings, you can try and make your buys over the phone. If you see some pieces you like in your local store, simply make a note of the relevant information (manufacturer, model number, color) and track down the manufacturer in North Carolina. When you call, you may find that the manufacturer will not accept orders over the phone; in that case, you're out of luck. After all, getting involved in accepting and arranging for delivery of retail telephone orders increases the overhead that these businesses are trying to eliminate by selling direct. Nevertheless, you stand a fairly decent chance of being able to work something out with a manufacturer over the telephone, so I suggest trying. To receive a free *Furniture Shopping Guide,* contact the Hickory, North Carolina Convention and Visitor's Bureau at (800) 849-5093. This guide provides a list of the furniture discounters in the Hickory area, but be advised that there are furniture outlets throughout the state. If you're planning to buy by telephone, for larger orders you will usually be required to pay a deposit of at least 20 percent (and it may be higher).

 Remember that aesthetics will cost you more.

If you want to purchase furniture that has a very unique look to it, perhaps something that involves a fancy cut to the wood, expect to pay a lot more for it. The differences can account for as much as 35 to 40 percent between two pieces of furniture that are functionally identical. My suggestion would be to find a piece that you like but that doesn't go overboard as far as incorporating a clever design.

*Save bucks by learning
how to handle the salesperson.*

Furniture salespeople can be the toughest nuts to crack of any. They can be just as motivated and hard-selling as the most formidable car salesperson, so watch out. They will oftentimes try to sell you more than you're looking for, in an attempt to up the store's take, as well as their own. Once again, commission-based compensation structures conspire to make life miserable for consumers. You don't, however, have to give in. Whether or not you do depends entirely on keeping your wits about you and staying focused on purchasing no more than the items you really need.

First of all, don't buy the fabric protection warranty that many salespeople will pitch when you buy an upholstered piece. The warranty can cost as much as $100, but it really won't do anything for you. If the fabric in your piece is man-made, those fibers will ward off stains with no other assistance. If the fibers are natural, they will have already been treated at the mill. If you do think you would benefit from some additional protection, then by all means invest in a can of Scotchgard™ so you can treat the fabric yourself.

Additionally, be wary of the salesperson's attempt to "upsell" you. This means either his or her attempt to get you to buy a piece you really cannot afford or trying to get you to buy additional pieces beyond those for which you came in.

I don't really have any strategy you can use to rebuff the salesperson when he tries to sell you something you know you can't afford. The best bet would be to just say no thanks. However, if you do buy it anyway, there's really no way to turn something like that into much of a positive. However, it *is* possible to turn his attempt at selling you additional pieces into a way to save money. Once you've decided that, yes you really need or want the extra items, go ahead and turn the tables on the salesperson, so that you can work him like he's working you. When he pitches you about buying another piece to go with the one you've already selected, tell him that you'll bite if he can offer you a substantial discount. If he says, no, then fine, you weren't really planning to purchase the item, anyway. However, if he's willing to knock 10 to 20 percent off of the listed price, then go for it. Either he will stop pressuring you or you'll walk out of the place with a better deal.

 Buy your furniture used and get top quality for rock-bottom prices.

It is my experience that buying used furniture is the very best deal around. There is little else out there that you can buy used that offers the same degree of value. If the furniture was treated well by the previous owner (and you shouldn't purchase it if it wasn't), then for all intents and purposes you are really purchasing a new piece of furniture for a used price. Furniture is the one type of expensive yet durable good that does not have the potential to wear out or break down quickly. The only problem with purchasing your furniture used is that the best opportunities will be found among private citizens; this can be a problem because you will almost always be in the position of having to pay cash for your purchases. If you can do that, it's likely that you will be able to get a good deal.

 Buy your furniture out of the Sunday classified section.

One of the best places to look for anything used is in the classified section of your newspaper. For the greatest selection, don't bother looking at any day except Sunday. Sunday papers are the most widely read, which is one of the reasons their classified sections are huge. You will find a substantial number of furniture ads in there, representing a wide variety of types and styles. You will probably have to call a lot of ads and visit a lot of people to find the things you want, but it will be well-worth your time. It is quite possible to furnish your entire home with quality furniture that cost as much as 80 percent less than its retail counterpart. It is not unusual to find used pieces, in some cases very old pieces, that are in substantially the same condition they were in when new.

When you shop the classifieds, you will often find people who are selling their furniture for peanuts because they're moving, have recently purchased new furniture, or have another reason that allows them to feel good about selling their goods for a lot less than they're worth. Granted, you will also find the ads of those who recognize the value of quality used furniture and will try to get as much as they can for it, but the neat part is that it's possible in the very next ad you peruse to find someone who is selling basically the same piece for a lot less. Personal circumstances often set the prices for people who are selling furniture, which is why there can be a tremendous disparity in prices.

 Arrive early at the flea market to snag a great deal.

Flea markets can be wonderful places to find bargains, and that's as true with furniture as anything else. With furniture, there's an additional strategy you can employ that may help you strike an even better deal.

Flea market dealers have to get to where they need to be very early in the day, long before the market actually opens. Motivated shoppers know this and will arrive early to begin finding their bargains. However, there's more to this than just getting first crack at the best merchandise. By arriving at least one hour before the market opens, you can oftentimes find the dealers making their goods available in the parking lot. Why? Well, furniture is big and heavy. If they can avoid having to move it to their specific sale site, they'll do so . . . even if it means giving a discount on what is already cut-rate stuff. Should you come across a dealer pushing his wares like this, try to work a deal that is roughly 15 percent below what it would otherwise be sold for. The dealer will not be excited about parting with an additional 15 percent, but he may do it if it means he doesn't have to lug the stuff around.

 Hit the garage sales with negotiating in mind.

Garage sales are also places to find furniture steals. Interestingly, though, many people will price their merchandise higher than it probably should be. The reason for this is that those holding garage sales know they will be bargained with, so they give themselves a head start, of sorts. Your strategy is to "step up to the plate" and offer about two-thirds less than what is being asked. You will usually find that you can walk away from the deal with a savings of 20 percent off the original asking price. Even though those holding garage sales want to make some money, they are also concerned with having to leave the unsold merchandise out for the garbage collector.

Appliances

Oftentimes, when people start identifying the kinds of items that are representative of what has become known as the "good life," appliances usually make it on the list somewhere. Appliance technology has allowed us to enjoy our lives so much more than people used to. The convenience and pleasure brought to us by washers, dryers, refrigerators, ovens, and dishwashers is sometimes tough to appreciate because so many of us these days have never been without these things.

Ask someone who has been without the above-mentioned goods, and then was able to possess them, how the quality of his or her life has changed as a result of coming to own these appliances. I have and, in responding, sometimes people have been reduced to tears, so great is their appreciation for being able to finally own these marvels of modern convenience.

Appliances are not cheap by any means. However, the good news is that with appliances, as with so many other high-dollar durable goods, there can be many opportunities to secure substantial discounts.

In this section, we're going to take a good look at a number of the very viable ways you can save a fortune on your appliance-shopping ventures. As with most opportunities to save money, on appliances it is oftentimes more a matter of paying attention and being willing to expend some effort than it is anything else. Some of this material can be categorized as common sense, but the truth is that very few people practice the strategies we're about to discuss. Let's get started saving money on appliance shopping!

 Know that you don't have to pay sticker price.

Buying appliances is not a lot different than buying cars, or even homes for that matter; there is a lot of room for negotiation. However, appliance retailers are very good at presenting their wares in such a fashion so as to suggest that your only choice is to pay the listed sticker price. Well, they can suggest all they want, but the reality is that there is ample space between an appliance's wholesale price and its retail price. In fact, the mark-up has been known to be as high as 100 percent. Do not be swayed by the salesperson's demeanor, the way a store presents its items, or the general public's long-held misperception that listed prices for appliances are non-negotiable. The mark-up on these kinds of goods is substantial and, depending on factors like current store-to-store competition, inventory levels, demand for the given items, and the salesperson's quota requirements (and his ability to meet them), you may be able to walk away from your appliance-shopping experience with an outstanding deal. The first step, though, is knowing that you *can*. Once you know that, you can focus on the variety of ways of securing that great deal.

Demonstrate to the salesperson that you've shopped around.

Here we go again—shopping around for a better deal. It works. In this case, your strategy will be to take advantage of the long-standing tradition in the retail appliance business of giving the customer a break if he can prove he's found the same item for less elsewhere. Many retailers will honor this tradition, but insiders will tell you that the retailer will make you work for the discount, rather than just handing it over.

What does "work for the discount" mean? It means that you have to prove that you have, in fact, found the appliance in question for less somewhere else. It is not enough to simply say that you found the item for less . . . you must be able to prove it. Make sure that you clip out the newspaper ads that showcase the appliance for which you're looking. Take the lowest-price ad you can find and use it as your bargaining chip when you enter another appliance retailer's establishment. Present the ad to the salesperson, and ask him if he can beat that price. If he can't beat it, then your next step is to see the manager. The manager will have a lot more leeway when it comes to giving discounts. If he can't get the deal done for you, then you might as well buy the appliance from the place that ran the ad in the first place. It would, however, be surprising if you were completely turned aside in your bid for a lower price.

What you are looking for is a discount of up to 10 percent off the sticker price. More would be great, of course, but I wouldn't expect to find more than that. Remember that whenever you're negotiating, you have two foes: the salesperson is one, of course, and the other is all the people who will enter the store prepared to pay the full retail price for the appliance. While retailers may be willing to give you a small reward in exchange for finally agreeing to purchase the product from them, they won't cut off much more than 10 percent because they know there are consumers out there who will not negotiate on the price.

 Save by purchasing last year's model.

An excellent purchase strategy is to buy the previous year's model. It is possible to receive an excellent deal on a car this way, and this holds true for appliances.

This savings strategy is especially suited for those people who do not feel the need to have the "latest and greatest" of everything. If practicality is your watchword, then you should be thrilled with the prospect of getting a good deal on a new appliance that may not have all the new features, but still serves the purpose for which it is intended with distinction. You should be able to realize a savings of up to 25 percent by going with a last year's "new" model instead of purchasing the newest version available.

When in the market for a new appliance, call some area retailers to find out when they expect the next year's model line to arrive (it will vary from make to make). Make a note of that general date, and then begin shopping at that time. You will find that the salespeople will be charged by management with the responsibility of, among other things, moving out the old inventory to make room for the new. At this point you may find that the old inventory will be priced to move, so there should already be some savings available. However, I suggest asking for another 10 to 25 percent off, depending on if the item is already being discounted. If it is, go for the 10 percent, but if it doesn't seem to have been repriced to help its liquidation, ask for the 25 percent. You may not actually do the deal at 25 percent off, but you should be able to leave with no less than 15 percent off the retail price. If the salesperson doesn't bite, then it's probably time to keep looking around because you will eventually find an appliance retailer who will oblige you.

Beware of purchasing front-loading washing machines.

When you set out to buy a washing machine, you may be looking at front-loading machines, like the kind you see in laundromats. The biggest claim to fame with these kinds of machines is that they run very efficiently. While it's true they use only about half the water of top-loading machines, they are priced much higher . . . usually several hundred dollars higher. Beyond the issue of higher price, these machines have a terrible record of durability, breaking down about twice as often as their top-loading counterparts.

Clean the coils in your refrigerator each month.

Unbeknownst to many, those coils that are located at the back of your refrigerator *do* serve a purpose, and when they become dirty or dusty your system must work a lot harder to do its job of keeping food cold. To help improve efficiency and cut costs, clean those coils each month with a vacuum cleaner. By following this simple procedure, you should be able to increase your refrigerator's operating efficiency by 25 percent.

*Save a lot by going
with a simple refrigerator model.*

Refrigerators come in a variety of sizes and sport many features. They are expensive appliances to buy as well as operate. Therefore, you may want to try to keep your costs way down by purchasing a relatively basic model. Side-by-side and bottom freezer refrigerators cost considerably more than the basic top freezer style, by anywhere from $150 to $500. Additionally, the top freezer models don't use as much energy as the other two. Be sure to pass on things like ice makers. Although ice makers add a measure of convenience, the cost they add both to the purchase price as well as to the on-going operating of the unit makes them cost-inefficient for the most part. Ice makers will typically add at least $100 to the cost of a refrigerator and as much as $50 to its monthly operation. Finally, units with ice makers need to be serviced about twice as often as those without.

Go appliance shopping in October.

If possible, wait to do your appliance shopping in October. Why? October is national kitchen and bath month, and you'll find all sorts of deals during that time. You should be able to save an additional 15 percent by purchasing your new appliances during this time.

*Buy used appliances
to secure solid value.*

I have an employee who, when I discussed this section of the book with him, raved about his washing machine. Apparently, when he was first married, he and his wife had very little money. They were able to buy a house, but didn't have much left over with which to furnish it and purchase appliances. It turns out that his wife knew someone who was a former repairman for a well-known brand of appliances who was retired but still reconditioned old units and resold them for some extra money. Well, these two purchased a washer and dryer from this fellow for a total of $150. That was seven years ago. Both units are still running today, and my employee has said that he has no interest in purchasing newer models until these finally give out. Oh, yes, and he said that since he's had them, each unit has needed to be serviced only one time.

Once again we see that buying expensive, durable goods in the aftermarket can mean big savings. In the case of washers and dryers, many repair-people believe that the older models are considerably better than the newer ones. Apparently, they go out on service calls almost twice as often for the newer models than they do for the older ones. The repair-people I have spoken to said this was frequently due of deference to the fact that newer appliances break down because, in order to run more efficiently, a unit has to be made with more delicate, finely made parts that are prone to damage. Older units, while perhaps not quite as energy-efficient, are built much sturdier. Remember, a service call from an appliance technician can be very expensive—even if the actual repair is simple.

There are a lot of ways you can locate quality used appliances. First, consider the Sunday classified section of your newspaper. As with furniture, you should be able to find excellent deals offered by private owners who are getting rid of their units. Alternatively, look in your Yellow Pages under "Appliances" and "Appliance Repair." You will see a lot of places that advertise used and reconditioned units. What's more, many of these places will warranty what they sell for a period of time, so you may want to take that into consideration.

Don't pay the repairman's service or trip charge.

If your unit has problems, you will need the services of a repairman (unless you're very handy yourself). There is a lot of competition in the appliance repair business, so use that to your advantage. Do not pay a service, or trip, charge if you actually have the unit fixed. Make that a condition of the call. Appliance repair services will frequently be quick to hit you with a $40 charge just for coming out to your home. While it may be easy to understand why a charge like this should be paid if you elect not to have any work done, there is no way you should pay it if you have the repairman work on your appliance(s). When you call to have someone come out, ask about the service's policy regarding trip or service charges. *Bottom line:* If the repairman with whom you speak on the phone isn't willing to drop service or trip charges if you end up having the unit repaired, keep looking for a repair service that will waive that charge.

Don't buy the service contract.

Whenever you buy a new appliance, you will be offered the opportunity to buy a service contract. These service contracts can add as much as $100 to the cost of your appliances. I advise against their purchase. First of all, your unit should be warrantied by the manufacturer for at least a year. This time period is significant because statistics show that if a unit makes it through the first year without a problem its chances of breaking down with a problem that would be covered by a warranty or service contract drop dramatically.

Instead of spending your money on a service contract, why not put a little bit of money aside each month toward a general cash reserve or emergency fund? By doing this you create a reservoir of money you can use if your appliances break down—and if they *don't* have any problems, you're creating a valuable resource to use if you have any other reason to need some quick cash.

5

Saving Money on Home and Yard Maintenance

My first real-estate purchase was a 600-square-foot condominium in Kissimmee, Florida. My mortgage payment was $202 per month! Now, three kids later, we're still in Florida but we live in a four bedroom home. I am not a handyman, which my wife can tell you firsthand. I thank our handymen over the years for sharing with me the ideas and strategies you will find in this chapter, as well as Bob Vila for the few times I caught his show.

If you're a homeowner, you've probably done your share of upkeep to both the structure and the yard. Even if you haven't been maintaining your property yourself, you have probably been paying someone to care for it. Our homes represent one of us our biggest investments. Into what other investment are you *required* to invest hundreds, even thousands, of dollars? With that kind of an investment, who wouldn't want to make sure that the condition of the investment is kept in top-flight condition?

Even if you never looked at your property as an investment vehicle, you still have to put a lot of time, effort, and money into it in order to keep it livable through the years. While there's not much of a way to get around putting a lot of the first two into your property, it is possible to save a substantial amount of money in the process of maintaining your residence. The best part is that saving money does not even require much of a knack for handiwork. You don't need to be a contractor to save a lot of money in all phases of home upkeep.

What we're going to talk about will enhance your financial circumstances with respect to your home in a variety of ways. Some of these strategies are designed to increase your home's value; others are designed to cut your costs of using your home; and still others are about saving money on the services you need performed on your home from time to time. Overall, it's all about putting (keeping?) more of your money in your pocket.

Keeping Your Home Temperate

Other than your mortgage, the biggest expense you will typically have each month will be your energy costs. The price to cool and heat a home can be steep, especially if you live in climes that are subject to extremes. However, keeping those costs down doesn't require much expense or "elbow grease," and the savings can be substantial. As you read on, you'll be amazed at just how small an investment is required to yield a great return.

 Keep your use of ventilation systems to a minimum.

If your bathroom or kitchen comes with a ventilation system to help keep those areas free and clear of odors, pay close attention to how you use the systems. If you allow them to run for too long, it's quite possible that in addition to clearing out the offensive odors, they will rid your home of the temperate air your heating/cooling system worked so hard to produce. When that happens, you will have to repeat the process of heating/cooling the house all over again. My advice is to go ahead and use those ventilation systems, but run them for only a few minutes.

 Make sure your attic is properly insulated.

This can save you a bundle and is probably the single most money-saving move you can make with respect to saving energy in your home. Insulation, by most estimates, can save a homeowner as much as 20 to 40 percent on heating and cooling costs. This is an excellent example of a small investment creating a substantial return. Depending on factors like the size of your attic and the type of insulation you choose, insulating this area can cost from $200 to $500. That's not cheap, to be sure, but let's say that your electric bill is currently averaging $100 per month. Even if we assume that you spent the maximum to insulate (about $500) and saved the minimum (about 20 percent), you would break even in about two years, which means that from the break-even point forward, you're keeping your money in your pocket.

To insulate, you can choose to do it yourself or have an insulation contractor do the work for you. Do-it-yourselfers will have to stick with using the type of insulation that comes either rolled or in the form of boards. Professionals often use the kind of insulation that is actually a foam that's blown into the rafters. Insulation is gauged in "R-value." If the R-value number is higher, that means the insulation is more effective. You will probably want to find out the R-value that's suggested in the area in which you live by stopping into a local Home Depot or other home improvement location and inquiring or calling your city's building and planning department. Get this information before you begin. As for how long the job will take . . . you should be able to finish it up in several hours.

*Be sure to change
your furnace filter regularly.*

If you own a furnace, get in the habit of replacing your furnace filter from time to time. Dirty furnace filters, like any other kind of filters lead to reduced efficiency and may cause problems for the system they're trying to protect if you leave them in too long. Fortunately, furnace filters are very inexpensive. You will save considerably over the course of many years if you change the filters properly. If you replace your furnace filter every four months, you can be sure to save 10 to 20 percent in overall energy costs. And always install new filters before the winter season begins.

Pests

Depending on where you live in the United States, you may be spending a small fortune to control pests. Pest control has become big business in this country; one look in the Yellow Pages reveals copious numbers of pest control companies that promise to deliver all sorts of services for a variety of fees.

If you like to spend money for the sake of spending money, fine. If not, consider doing some things that can reduce or even eliminate your professional pest control bill altogether. By following the strategies I'm going to present to you in this section, you should be able to take a large step toward cutting your pest control expenses substantially.

*Consider do-it-yourself
pest control.*

Although many people wouldn't dream of doing it, the fact is that there are many excellent products that are available over-the-counter which you can use to control the pest problems you have. The biggest reason people don't choose this option is clearly the hassle involved. If you've ever seen pest control people at work, you know they get into every nook and cranny to treat all areas of your home. That can be a chore. This is especially true when you realize that most over-the-counter pest control formulas are not of the same strength (and thus, don't have the same degree of longevity) as those used by the pros, which means you'll have to treat your home more frequently. Nevertheless, you can save thousands of dollars over the years by treating your home yourself.

 Take steps now to prevent costly termite problems.

Although they are especially plentiful in states that have warmer climates (particularly my home state, Florida), termites can get a hold of you just about anywhere (except Alaska, or so I've been told by experts). Although you can wait to fight the ravenous critters after they've attacked, it's much healthier for your wallet and your house if you take some steps beforehand to help ensure that termites don't become a major problem.

One thing you should never do is allow things like wooden fences and woodpiles to run so close to the house that they touch the structure. When exterior wood like that is positioned right next to your home, you are giving termites easy access to your most valuable possession. Play it safe, and be sure there is always some daylight between your home and your woodpile, or your home and your wooden fence.

Speaking of exterior wood, you should know, as well, that the best thing you can do to prevent termites is to have all exterior wood structures treated by a pest-control professional. This treatment is not at all expensive, and can save you hundreds, even thousands, in the long run. This will be especially important if you are building an add-on structure, like a porch or deck, to your home or you're installing an overhang of some kind that will be supported by wooden beams. No matter what you're doing, you will be best served by arranging to have the wood treated by a professional as quickly as possible. I realize that I just suggested do-it-yourself pest control in the previous section, but this is a good example of where not to try and scrape by. This treatment of exterior wooden surfaces will cost you very little, no more than $50, even if done by a professional. It will, however, be your smartest move overall as you add wood structures to your home now and through the years.

 Control fleas with diatomaceous earth.

If you have pets, chances are you have fleas. These little critters are amazingly annoying and cause tremendous discomfort to your dog or cat. What's more, a flea infestation in your home can be a real embarrassment if they take a liking to your guests. There is nothing that says "yuck!" quite like a bunch of fleas jumping on you or a guest as soon as you sit down in a big cushy chair or lie on the carpet.

Fleas can be controlled, to be sure, but some methods of dealing with them are clearly superior to others. I can tell you now, though, that if you are utilizing the kinds of flea control treatments that require you to chase the little guys around, then you are wasting valuable energy and money—and probably not helping the problem nearly as well as you could. Sprays and shampoos have some measure of effectiveness, but the problem is that unless you kill every last one, the problem will usually return. Flea "bombs" can be excellent, as they allow for the entire interior of the home to be treated in one shot. However, bombs can be a real inconvenience since you must prepare your residence and then leave it for a period of time while the chemicals are spreading throughout the home.

If you want a much easier way to deal with fleas, simply make a trip to your local yard-and-garden supply store and buy a powder called diatomaceous earth, or DE. DE has a crystalline makeup that penetrates the waxy coating on fleas as they come in contact with it. Without this waxy coating, the fleas will "dry out" and die, which is precisely what DE will *make* them do. What's nice about this kind of treatment is that it is much less hassle than using more traditional methods of flea control *and* the cost of DE is very minimal. You should be able to buy a year's worth of DE for about $10. When you apply DE *light* to the surface areas of your home (not all of them, mind you, just the corners and such), you should find that your flea problem will disappear.

One note: Diatomaceous earth comes in different densities. Make sure you do not get the DE that is really fine, like that sold in pool supply stores; DE can be dangerous if inhaled; therefore, the finer it is, the likelier this is to happen.

Wipe out cockroaches
with cucumbers and bay leaves.

Cockroaches are disgusting. There's no two ways about it. If anyone knows of a reason why I should not feel that way, please let me know. There's nothing quite like flipping on the kitchen light in the middle of the night to search for a drink or snack and seeing a roach or two scurry across your floor and back into some hiding place that most of us can't reach. Little else will take your appetite away as quickly.

When people pay for professional extermination services, they are oftentimes doing so in an effort to rid themselves of a roach problem. Few other pests are as motivating. However, do not feel obligated to make the "bug man" a permanent recipient of your monthly bill outflow. There is actually a way you can handle the cockroach problem yourself very effectively for a lot cheaper than you may have ever thought possible.

Although it may sound a little hokey, you can keep cock-roaches away by slicing up a cucumber and placing the slices in areas where the little guys are known to congregate. It turns out that the chemical makeup of cucumbers is such that it keeps roaches away. Bay leaves are known to have the same effect, so make sure you place these natural alternatives to chemical treatment throughout the dark areas of your home, particularly your kitchens and bathrooms. You're getting rid of these house pests for the cost of a small salad!

General Home Maintenance

For most people, home repair jobs are either loved or hated. If you're the handy type, you'll approach these tasks with a certain amount of enthusiasm; if you're not, then you probably dread them and will look for someone else to do them for you. The vast majority of handy jobs required to keep a home looking good and running well are really quite simple to perform. The key lies in knowing what you can do to help save money and enhance the value of your home. This section will help the handy types see which jobs deserve real priority, and will also help those who hire professionals to save money in that endeavor, too.

 Hire painters near or during winter months.

The painting business is a very seasonal one. During spring and summer months, painters are usually hopping all over the place to keep up with the demand for their services. Accordingly, if you think you're going to receive a bargain during this time, you're dreaming (and if you run across someone who *does* offer to paint your home very cheaply during those seasons, you may want to be cautious because quality painters will be commanding premium rates for their services then). The key to saving, as it is in so many cases when you're looking to hire service people, is to identify their slow season and do your hiring then.

Most people don't think about hiring painters during the late fall and winter months. First of all, those months are usually the ones when we are busiest with work and school responsibilities, and thoughts of painting the house just don't enter our minds. Second, and most importantly, the fall and winter seasons are hardly conducive to exterior painting jobs.

Nevertheless, these can be excellent times to hire. If you live more northward, you may be limited in how many of these off-season months you have at your disposal; you certainly can't have your home's exterior painted in a snowstorm or when it is biting cold. However, during early-to-mid fall, as well as late winter, you should find that the climate may cooperate long enough for you to feel comfortable hiring an exterior painter. If you live more southward, you will have more flexibility. In Florida, for example, you can hire an exterior house painter all year long. Wherever you live, you should be able to realize a significant discount off premium rates when you hire in the off-season. You should be able to pocket at least a 25 percent savings, and my research has found that you can sometimes save as much as 40 percent.

Interestingly, you can also save on interior jobs as well. Although you might not expect that to be so because outdoor climate conditions shouldn't matter to interior painting efforts, I've found that all kinds of house painting jobs are pricier in the spring and summer, and much less during the fall and winter. As to why this is with even interior jobs, the answer in this case has more to do with work and school commitments than with the weather conditions. People also don't think about having this kind of work done, especially over the course of months that are occupied by several holidays. The savings on interior jobs can be as great as those on exterior jobs.

Does your house really need repainting—or just a good wash?

I wasn't aware how dirty a home's exterior could get until I had a portion of my house pressure cleaned. When the fellow was done, it honestly looked like the house had been repainted; I kid you not. I then did some digging, and sure enough, research confirms that pressure washing a home oftentimes makes it look like it had just been professionally painted. The savings between the two is extraordinary. If you usually hire exterior painters, then you may save thousands of dollars, depending on the size of your home. If you're a do-it-yourself painter, the financial savings won't be as great (renting a pressure washer for a day costs about half as much as the supplies to repaint), but the savings in time and effort will be tremendous.

Of course, if your home truly needs to be repainted then pressure washing is a poor substitute. In fact, it might make your problem worse because if the paint on your home is cracking and peeling, pressure washing will intensify that problem enormously (which is why most professional painters use high-pressure cleaning systems to help prepare the surface beforehand). However, a quality exterior paint job should last at least five years, so if you're looking at your home before then and thinking it needs to be painted again, look more closely—maybe all it needs is a good cleaning.

If you do the painting yourself, spend more on materials to realize a greater savings in the long run.

Saving money by deriving value is not the same thing as going out and paying a cheap price for something. In fact, simply focusing on the bottom line without regard to how your money is truly being spent frequently ends up costing you a lot more. This strategy is going to be another example of how spending more money initially will save you *a lot* more down the road.

If you've decided to paint your home yourself, your biggest expense will be the cost of materials. There is a wide variety of each type of material from which to choose—from paint, to brushes, to rollers, to caulk, to sanding equipment. Do yourself a big favor and spend the extra money to obtain the highest-quality materials you can. The most important item in this regard is paint. A poor-quality paint will begin to fade, crack, and peel after just a few years. As stated previously, your home should not need to be painted any more often than every five years or so, so make sure you've selected a quality of paint that will allow you to stick to that schedule. Top quality paints are not that much more expensive than mediocre quality paints, and choosing them will likely extend by 50 to 100 percent the amount of time that will elapse between required paint jobs.

Paint is not the only consideration, either. If you choose lower-quality paints, rollers, and paint brushes, you may find yourself painting bristles onto your home with the paint and wasting time correcting the uneven cover jobs that cheap rollers cause. Also, poor-quality caulks and wood patches won't seal and adhere properly. Don't be too cheap for your own good. If you have decided to paint on your own, you're already going to save a fortune. Now, spend the little bit of additional money that will be required to ensure you won't have to paint your home more often.

 Save a bundle on roofing by "partnering" with the roofing contractor.

If you've had to replace the roof of your home recently, you are probably still smarting from the bite the whole job took out of your wallet. Roofing jobs can cost anywhere from several hundred dollars for minor repairs to well over $10,000 for a new roof, depending on the size of your home. Because roofing jobs can be so expensive, there is room to save a lot of money—perhaps cut your costs by half—but you will have to be willing to do a substantial amount of the work yourself.

"Now wait," you may be thinking, "I'm no roofing specialist, and this kind of work is serious business." True enough, but I'm not going to suggest that you do the more specialized roofing chores yourself. Instead, you can save yourself a lot of money if you resolve to do the part of the job that requires some effort but not much skill.

If you need a new roof, have the roofing contractor do the really tough and important stuff, like removing the old roof and installing the new sheathing and building paper. Then, you can come along and install the shingles yourself. Just doing that part of the job on your own will save you as much as half off a complete roofing job—and half-off can mean thousands of dollars.

If you've never done this kind of work or it's been a long time, I suggest that you refer to any of the excellent resources available to do-it-yourselfers. Many home improvement centers like Home Depot sell books and other reference sources that are designed to help novices successfully complete all types of home repair jobs. There is a lot of help available in this area, so take the time to do a little homework *before* you talk to a contractor so that you know in advance how feasible it is for you to participate in reroofing your home.

When you seek bids from roofing contractors, be sure to find out what you can do to keep the cost of the job down. Don't be concerned that the contractors will wince at the thought of giving up some of their potential return in order to keep your costs down. They will likely welcome the opportunity to include you in the process because doing so means they can move on to the next job much more quickly.

Install flow restrictors to keep your water costs down.

A quick and easy way you can save a lot of money on the use of your water is to install flow restrictors in faucets and shower heads. Flow restrictors are little mechanisms that more efficiently regulate the outflow of water, and the best part is that you barely notice the difference in the flow rate. However, you should notice a sizable difference in the amount of your water bills. You can save 25 to 35 percent each month on hot water costs by installing these handy-dandy little devices. What's more, they're simple to install and it only takes a few minutes.

Save on the cost of a new bathtub by repainting your old one.

A quality new bathtub can cost a lot of money. If you're in the market for a new one, you should ask yourself why. A bathtub should last forever—or nearly forever—making buying a new one unnecessary. The purchase and installation of a new bathtub can run into thousands of dollars, so unless you absolutely have to have a new one go ahead and pass.

If the reason you want a new one has to do with the *appearance* of the old one, that can be fixed for a lot less than the amount you'll spend on a new tub. I suggest you have the old one repainted; yes, repaint it. I realize you may not have heard that suggestion, but doing it can save you a lot of money. I'm not necessarily suggesting that you do the repainting yourself, but even if you pay a professional you'll still save oodles of dough. To have a tub professionally repainted, you may spend a few hundred dollars. Compare that with $1,000 or more to purchase a new one and have it installed.

Install a timer
on your hot water heater.

Hot water heaters can take a lot out of our monthly budgets—much more than we may realize. The purpose of these conveniences is to heat water, obviously, but do you have any idea how frequently they are actually heating? All of the time. Between the uses demanded by dishwashers, washing machines, showers, and regular faucets, the hot water heater is rarely shut off for very long, usually no more than a few minutes at best. Keeping this in mind, it makes a lot of sense to install a hot water heater timer. These timers see to it that your hot water heater is running only during the night, when rates are the least expensive. By the time the water heater shuts off in the morning, you should have more than enough hot water to last for the rest of the day. By sticking with this kind of timing schedule, you may be able to slash your hot water costs by more than 30 percent—not bad savings. You can pick up a hot water heater timer at any home improvement center, and either install it yourself or pay a few bucks to have a pro do it for you. Either way, your savings in the long run should be tremendous.

Lawn and Yard Maintenance

Most experts will tell you that the easiest and cheapest way to increase the value of your home is to put time, money, and effort into landscaping it. It is amazing to see the same residence before any appreciable landscaping is done, and then again after the work is complete. It's possible to change the outside appearance so dramatically, that a second look is required by those already familiar with the home to convince them that they are looking at the same residence as before. Here's a clue: If you've ever seen something as simple as a lawn well-maintained, versus one that is not maintained, and notice how much difference there is on the overall appearance of the home's exterior, then imagine what kind of difference genuine landscaping efforts can make.

The really nice thing about lawn and general yard maintenance is that you don't have to have any special knack to be able to do it. In fact, yard care and landscaping is maybe the one area of home maintenance that most people can perform well because they don't need to be electrically inclined, mechanically inclined, handy with tools, or anything like that. The most important requirement for making and keeping the yard looking good is to have a good eye; that is, to be able to identify what improvements will look good where. If you can do that, the rest is easy. There are many landscape articles, magazines, and books that can be found at home-improvement stores, your local library, and on the Internet.

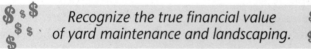

Recognize the true financial value of yard maintenance and landscaping.

There is probably no other more cost-effective way to enhance the value of your home and provide the satisfaction that comes from living on a well-maintained property than landscaping. Most ornamental bushes and trees, flowers, and so on are very cheap to buy and, properly installed around the home, can make a huge impact on appearance. Annual flowers are just a few dollars each, and many small bushes and trees can be had for as little as $15 or $20 a piece. What's more, it is generally understood among real estate experts that you add $2 in value to your residence for every $1 that you spend. One thousand dollars spent on sprucing up your property with lawn, garden, and other collateral area work will translate, then, to a $2,000 increase in your home's value. Where else can you go to realize a 100 percent return on your investment? Get serious about this task; it will undoubtedly be one of the smartest expenditures of time and money you could possibly make on your home.

Do your planting in the fall.

Most people plant trees, bushes, and the like in the spring. Call it spring fever or whatever you want, but most people don't see the point of planting just before winter comes. That, however, is a mistake. First of all, products at nurseries and lawn-and-garden centers cost a lot less money in the fall than in the spring. The reason is that with winter approaching, these places are anxious to move out their remaining stock as quickly as possible. It's possible to save as much as 50 percent on the same trees and bushes in the fall that you would normally buy in the spring.

Interestingly, too, many lawn-and-garden experts recommend doing your planting in the fall months. The transplanting process will naturally slow the growth of these trees and bushes. Therefore, by doing it as the winter months approach (when these things will be dormant anyway), they'll not be as far behind in the growth cycle when spring finally comes around and the growing season returns full-tilt.

 Ask for a discount whenever you buy trees and bushes in bulk.

Nurseries and lawn-and-garden centers like to move their inventory quickly because they deal with living things that will not thrive in retail environments. It is in their best interests to sell them as quickly as possible, making room for the fresher plants. Because of this, always seek a discount when you buy in larger quantities. If you're buying trees, for example, you should ask for a discount of around 25 percent per tree after you've purchased the first few at full-price. You should be able to realize some measure of a discount, even if it's not the 25 percent, but if you don't like the deal you're offered at one place, there's always others you can go to.

Install a gauge on lawn sprinklers
to limit unnecessary water use.

Lawn sprinklers are certainly the most convenient watering methods you can own. One problem is that sprinklers generally work off of a timer, so there is a chance they will still run even if the ground has been soaked with rain. Do away with that kind of wastefulness; go to a local home-and-garden center and buy a gauge that will automatically prevent sprinklers from running if the ground is already wet. You should pay no more than $20 for this device, and it will save you a great deal of money over time. This is especially true in places like Florida that get a lot of rain in the late-spring to early-fall months.

To save money, don't use sod.

Sod looks wonderful. It is a ready-made lawn transplanted to your yard. However, you pay dearly for that convenience. Instead, why not go through the process of planting the lawn on your own with grass seed? The results aren't as immediate, but you will save a bundle depending on the size of the area you want to build. Your local lawn-and-garden in store is a great resource for information and instructions on growing grass.

Get your mulch for free from the town
or city in which you live.

It is not uncommon, as we drive around town doing our errands, to come across municipal maintenance workers clearing away underbrush, trees, and so on. We see the work being done, and even see them grind the refuse into mulch. So what happens to that mulch? Well, the fact is, you as a resident can have the city deliver a load of mulch to your property for you to use in your landscaping efforts. I discovered this as I checked into what, if any, services like this were available to resident homeowners within a community. Granted, mulch is not that expensive to begin with (in some areas, it's not much more than a dollar a bag), but you can't ever beat free, and free is what I'm talking about. Call your town or city's department of public works for more information.

6

Transportation Savings

I want to start this chapter by telling you that I drive a bright-red Corvette. There is a school of thought that says you can tell a lot about a person by the vehicle he or she drives. I don't know how true this thinking is, but I can tell you that I love cars, the faster the better. I can't bring myself to be very practical when it comes to the kind of car I get to drive everyday from my home to my office, which is just across the street from a Florida beach. There is no greater lunch break than to drive my Corvette up and down the beach. For most people, their automobiles will rival the cost of a small house. It is my goal in this chapter, to help you be practical and—yes—still have fun driving the car of your dreams.

Our discussion in this chapter is going to cover driving from A to Z. First, we're going to talk about strategies you can use to greatly lessen how much you pay for a new car. Next, we're going to talk about how to save money on a used car, and then follow that up with a discussion on how to cut your costs to lease a car, if you decide that leasing is more your speed. Following our discussions on the most cost-effective ways to get into the car of your choice, I will talk about two important collateral issues related to cars: saving money when you insure them and saving money when you have them serviced.

You can see, then, that we have a lot to talk about, so let's get right to it and see the absolutely amazing ways you can save money when you buy and use your vehicles.

Buying the New Car

Even though it's toughest to save money when you're seeking to buy a new car, many people want to have the newest model that comes off the assembly line. Although the best ways to save money on car purchases involve buying the vehicles used, I'm not going to try to convince you who have your heart set on a new car to buy anything else. What car to buy is a personal financial decision that is, hopefully, made after much research and forethought. Rather, I'm going to use this opportunity to help the prospective new car buyer make the best deal he or she can.

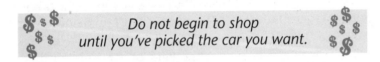

Do not begin to shop until you've picked the car you want.

One of the biggest mistakes many prospective buyers of new cars make is to begin the shopping process without having settled on the one make of car they want to purchase. Too many of us allow our heads to be turned by the latest, greatest models to come out of Detroit or wherever, which is fine as long as you settle down and pick a car to shop for before you start entering showroom floors.

Why is this so important? The car shopping process is a most challenging one, and it requires your undivided attention. You will be making excursions to a variety of dealerships and haggling with each one of them—and that's just when you shop for the same car at different locations. Make your life simple; do a lot of research *before* you begin your quest, and once you've decided on a make and model, *then* begin to shop in earnest. When you see how much energy and focus proper car shopping can take, you'll be glad that you disciplined yourself to the task of making your selection first.

 Learn the factory invoice price of the car you want.

Once you've decided on a car, you must now do the one thing that will give you the most important information you'll need with which to begin car shopping: Learn the invoice price of your dream machine.

Although the same new car will be priced differently, depending on the dealership you're at, the cars are actually all purchased at the factory for the same price by the car dealers. What you want to do is to learn that factory price, known as the "invoice price," so you can have a basis for comparison when you go from dealership to dealership. Too many people enter a dealership to negotiate on the price of a car and simply haggle off the sticker price indicated in the window. That's a big mistake because the sticker price is likely going to be way overpriced to begin with, so after you're done haggling off the sticker price, you may feel as though you earned a great deal, when in fact you still ended up paying a lot more than you should have. What you should do is go into the dealerships armed with the invoice price and negotiate from there. Now, be forewarned that you will not be negotiating down from that invoice price when new car shopping. There are too many people out there who will not be using these strategies for the dealer to just hand over a new car to you for below the invoice price (although it is possible to buy a new car for below invoice at rare times during the year).

However, with the invoice price in hand, you can comparison shop on the basis of price, knowing full well what each dealer paid for the car. Not only will that tell you whose sticker price is the best deal, but it allows you to negotiate the cost of the car down further—you will know what the dealer's cost is and will be able to negotiate intelligently from there.

So, how do you go about obtaining this magical invoice price number? It's not as difficult as you may think. In this age of increased consumerism, there are a number of excellent resources available to help you find the information you need. In my experience, the *Edmund's* series of car-pricing guides are among the most accurate and most thorough of those to be found anywhere. The *Edmund's* guides deliver not only detailed pricing information, including invoices prices, but also give excellent narrative reports on each car. These guides are available on everything from new cars, to used cars, to light trucks, to sport utility vehicles. You can pick them up at any decent bookstore, and what's more, they're published several times through the year to ensure that the most up-to-date information is available.

Whenever I'm asked what the single most important strategy to use when shopping for a new car is, my reply is to know the invoice price before you walk onto the dealership lot. If you follow no other strategy in this section, follow this one.

 Make loan arrangements before you make that trip to the dealership.

Although much has changed in recent years, car loans purchased through the dealership are still, in general, going to be your worst bet. Always arrange your financing *before* beginning your actual voyage to the dealerships. Dealer-arranged financing usually adds a point or two to what should be the "real" cost of your loan. (This is done so that the lender can compensate the dealer for steering you to them. It's another way that dealers can increase their profit margins at your expense.)

Normally, when you apply for a loan at a lender (other than the dealer's lender of choice), you will have 60 days to purchase your car before the loan term expires and you have to reapply. Because it shouldn't cost anything to apply for an auto loan, I suggest you apply for several of them and settle on the one that gives you the best bottom-line terms. Of course, the beauty of this is that, with loan in hand, you can shop with peace of mind, knowing that the financing issues have already been addressed. I do suggest listening to what the dealer has to say with respect to financing because they often offer loan incentive rates. Although rare, you may discover dealer financing is better than what you can obtain on your own.

 Know the best time to shop for a new car.

If someone has told you there are better times than others to shop for a new car, I want you to know that he or she was right. First of all, you want to save your best shopping efforts for the end of the day, as opposed to the beginning of the day. Car salespeople are no different than the rest of us; their days can be long, and as they tire, their willingness to strike a deal on a new car will rise substantially. Take advantage of that by arriving at the dealership later in the day and stretching the whole process out if you have to.

Second, there is also a better time of the month to do your car shopping. Monthly sales quotas, the backbone of the sales effort at car dealerships, must be met. If a salesperson is behind on his quota at the close of the month, he will be more likely to make a deal that takes more money out of his pocket and puts it back into yours. It's okay to shop for your car at any time of the day, but when you arrive at the dealership intent on making a deal, do it late in the day and close to the end of the month.

Last, there is a better time of the year to buy a car than at any other time. The funny thing is, it's the time of the year when it is usually the worst time to buy anything else from a consumer's standpoint. That's right—I'm talking about Christmas.

Car dealerships are virtually empty during the Christmas holidays. Oh, you'll see the ads that invite you to come in and buy that loved one a brand-new car for Christmas, but how many of us are in the position to seriously entertain that?

Shopping for a car during the Christmas season gives you a couple of advantages. First, as I've said, dealerships are very, very slow during that time of the year. Consumers are out at the malls or conserving their funds for the less-pricey gifts they'll be buying. Also, price aside, most people don't want to deal with the hassles of car shopping during this time of the year. Last, and very helpfully, the Christmas season also represents the time of year when dealers will do just about anything to rid themselves of the previous year's inventory. If you're smart and can wait, you'll go into the dealership at this time of the year not intending to buy one of the new model-year vehicles, but to purchase one of the previous year's new models.

That's how you enhance your savings when buying at this time of the year: You combine the advantages of being willing to enter the dealership during their slow season with your insistence to buy only a last year's "new" model. Chances are, they'll still have plenty of them left, and you should be able to work an amazing deal if you play your cards right. In fact, this is the one unique time of the year when it's actually possible to get the best deal. If a dealership is desperate enough to want to liquidate inventory, you may be able to walk away with your dream car for the invoice price . . . or perhaps even a little less.

"Less," you say? "It's possible to walk away with a new car for less than the invoice price?" Yes, it is. Dealers will receive a broad commission of about 5 percent of the invoice price of a car when they sell one. In other words, that kickback is already factored in to the invoice price the dealership pays, so it's possible for the dealer to sell the car for below invoice and still make a profit.

Never buy the car on your first visit to the dealership.

We've all experienced it: The feeling that comes with walking onto a lot where there are so many of the new and shiny cars we want so badly. We can't help ourselves . . . we become giddy with excitement and our hearts start beating faster. We see so many of what we want, and we want one *now*.

Hold on. One of the *worst* mistakes you can make is to do a deal on your first trip to the dealership. No matter what happens, resolve to leave that dealership without having made a purchase. (Hey, if they want to *give* you the car then you can make the deal, but short of that, plan to drive away in the car in which you arrived.)

Your tactic here is to make the salesperson hungry. Chat about the car, even go into his office and talk about the car—but get up and walk away. Now, please understand that numerous surveys have indicated that if you get up and leave, you'll never come back, which is why he will try to keep you captive. When he sees you go, he'll be very frustrated, which means that when he sees you return he'll be salivating even more. The more time you spend with him, the more time he's invested in the whole process. That makes it less likely that he will allow the deal to go undone, even if it means he has to forsake a sizable portion of his commission.

Bypass the no-haggle dealerships.

If you've been paying attention, you'll notice that more and more dealers are going the no-haggle route. This means that by agreeing not to engage in the hard-sell tactics for which the car sales industry is famous (and which invariably make the dealers beyond rich), they are able to charge a "fair," flat rate for the vehicles. Another feature of these dealerships is that the salespeople, long the source of problems for car consumers because of their thirst for commissions, are generally on a salary-based compensation structure. Many consumers regard the no-haggle style of dealership as a breath of fresh air and a step in the right direction as far as their wallets are concerned.

But do the no-haggle dealerships really give consumers a better deal than they can get on their own by negotiating? The short answer is no. Learned estimates suggest that at no-haggle dealerships, car buyers are paying an average of 12 percent above invoice price for the car, which in my opinion is way too much to be forking over. My suggestion is that you plan to pay anywhere from 1 to 5 percent above invoice, with 3 percent representing a nice average. With Americans paying an average of $20,000 for a new car, a 3 percent figure in that general area can represent a nice commission. At that rate, even if a salesperson sells just one car every other day on a five-day workweek, he can still earn around $75,000 per year.

One problem with the advent of this new style of dealership is that the average consumer thinks these new styles of dealership are the way to go. The fact remains that a shopper who is committed to haggling will generally fare much better than someone who is more concerned with enjoying a peaceful shopping experience.

 Stick to your guns about paying no more than 5 percent above invoice.

This goes back to that key bit of information known as the invoice price. As we've noted, commissions on cars will vary widely, but dealers all pay the same invoice prices. It's important to mention at this time that built in to that invoice price is a commission to the dealership itself. This structure can get somewhat clever, but the bottom line is that about 5

percent of the invoice price is actually retained by the dealership as a commission, which means that essentially what you're
haggling over is the salesperson's commission. Clearly, a salesperson has every right to a fair commission (especially when
you consider what you'll be putting him or her through), but
remember that until relatively recently, "fair" commissions
were considered to be well over 20 percent above invoice in
some cases. If you find yourself receiving a lot of static in your
efforts to pay no more than 3 to 5 percent above invoice, just
keep shopping around. You can try to cleverly negotiate down
to that price, but if that doesn't work have no fear of walking
into a dealership and announcing to the salesperson that you
know what you want to buy, and that the two of you may be
able to do a deal if he can produce an invoice for the car you
want that matches what you already know to be the invoice
price. Once you're happy with the invoice you've been given,
let him know that you'll pay X percent (you decide what that
figure should be) above that invoice price and no more. If he
takes your offer it may be the easiest sale he's ever made.

If you don't see a lot of other people engaging in this
strategy when they go car shopping, it's because they are either
unaware of how the system works or are unwilling to be as forward and to the point as one must sometimes be in order to
pull it off. However, now you know how it can be done so walk
into the dealership and make your announcement. Sooner or
later you should have what you want for the price you want.

 *Tell the dealer, "thanks,
but no thanks" on dealer costs.*

Whenever you go to buy a new car, you will find that there
are a lot of "dealer costs" on the sticker that you're expected
to pay. What are these costs?

First, there's the famous prep fee, which is basically the
charges for washing your new car before handing it over to

you. Any other preparations that are needed are covered in the basic cost of your new car, so you need to be persistent about your unwillingness to pay such fees. What else could you pay? There's the "dealer added profit." Sorry, but that's already built into the basic cost of the car. What about a "locator fee"? "The dealer had to go out of his way to locate the color I wanted, with the options I wanted, surely he should be paid something for his effort." Why? It's his job to sell cars, and part of selling cars involves making sure that he has the inventory on-hand to meet the demand of customers. There's no need to pay him extra for doing what he's supposed to do.

Now, I guarantee your salesperson will start to resist when you mention that you want out of all of these extra fees. It's his job to do that, but maintain your unwillingness to pay any of them. If you have been negotiating for a while with him, and raise these issues toward the end, it's much likelier that he will be more compliant with your wishes. Ultimately, whether or not you want these costs to be a deal-breaker, if it comes to that, is up to you. However, most dealers won't let these fees stand in the way of what will already be a substantial profit.

Used Cars

I have long been a fan of buying used instead of new. Although it can be very prudent to buy new when it comes to most things, when it comes to cars the decision is not even close. Cars are perhaps the worst offenders when it comes to goods that depreciate in value significantly once they've been purchased. Have we not all heard the adage that a car loses thousands of dollars in value once it's driven off the lot? During the first year of ownership, new cars will depreciate approximately 30 percent in value, and can easily depreciate another 15 to 20 percent in the second year. This means that after just two short years of new car ownership, your car, which may still be in near-perfect condition, is worth about half what you paid for it.

Those figures should be enough to convince anyone to consider buying used, but I realize there's going to be reluctance, particularly for those who feel that buying a used car is a risk. That fear is understandable, but the good news is that it's not as relevant as it once was. Not only are cars made much better now, but the used, or "preowned," car industry has seen a rebirth as the cost of new cars has risen substantially through the years. More and more professional dealerships that specialize in quality, late-model used cars have come into vogue, and warranties, once considered unheard of for used cars, are frequently available.

All in all, the market for quality used cars is excellent and getting better all the time. Let's look at some strategies you can use to help make a good deal substantially better.

 Buy a car that's two to three years old.

As I mentioned previously, after a two-year time period, it's hardly unusual for a car to have lost 50 percent of its original value. Nevertheless, a two-year-old car will probably still be in excellent condition if it has been diligently maintained. Even if the used car you're contemplating has as much as 60,000 miles on it, be advised that a mileage figure like that is not nearly as significant as it once was. There was a time when it was considered prudent to begin shopping for a new car as soon as your old car had 60,000 miles on it. Not anymore. Nowadays, 60,000 miles is nothing and, in fact, any late-model car that can't breeze past the 100,000-mile mark with ease is considered dysfunctional.

"If a two- to three year-old car is such a good deal, why not go for one even older and enhance the value?" The value begins to diminish after two years. The car's rate of depreciation begins to slow, but the rate of wear and tear tends to increase. The bottom line is that you don't want to buy new, but you don't want to buy too used in order to realize the best value overall.

Get a bigger bang for your buck
by shopping for a lease car.

No, this strategy does not recommend leasing (I'll talk about how to save money on leasing in a bit). What I'm saying here is that an excellent way to garner greater value in your used car purchase is to specifically shop for a car that was once a lease, or "program," vehicle. Why? The terms of leases are such that lessees normally don't have quite the same inclination to put high miles on a car that they might otherwise because leases come with mileage restrictions. Also, dealerships that lease cars require the lessees to keep the cars well maintained as part of the agreement. As a result, there is an additional, built-in measure of value that you can realize.

If you can, buy your used car
directly from the owner.

If you really want to save some money on a used car purchase, consider buying the vehicle directly from the previous owner. Since the selling of cars is not a business to them, individual owners will be more likely to offer the cars at prices that are more reflective of their true value at that time. Dealers, on the other hand, are out to make as substantial a profit as possible, so they will try to liquidate their inventory at prices that are typically 20 percent above a private owner's price.

Another excellent advantage to buying directly from the true owner is that you have ample opportunity to find out honestly about the quality of the vehicle. By engaging the owner in conversation, you will give him the opportunity to talk at length about the car, which he will likely enjoy doing (watch out, though; if he's very tight-lipped and chooses his words carefully that could be an indication that he has something to hide). Also, as far as bargaining goes, by dealing with a private individual, you're giving yourself a much better chance of walking away with the deal you really want because you won't be negotiating with an expert salesperson (at least, it's not likely that you'll be negotiating with one).

 If you can,
go to a professional auto auction.

If you want to get the deal of a lifetime, the auto auction is the place to be. Professional auto auctions are generally accessible only by individuals who possess dealer licenses, so if you want to go you need to find someone who can get you in. If you can get in, you'll find in short order that it is *the* place to buy a used vehicle. It is not unheard of for quality vehicles to go for as much as 50 percent less than their true value, and sometimes the savings can be even greater. The auction is where dealers go to obtain much of their inventory and, after one visit, it's easy to see why.

There are a couple of downsides, however, to going through the auction. First, auctions usually deal on a cash-only basis: no personal checks, no certified checks, no authorized lines of credit . . . only cash—as in greenbacks. Also, you're on your own at the auction when it comes to ensuring that the car is in proper working condition. Inventory issues also arise at auctions; it's hard to predict what will be made available for sale on the date you're going, so you have to take your chances. This instance may be the only one where I might back away from my previous statement that you should have one particular type of car to focus your efforts on. If you might go the auction route, it would be wise to have several candidates picked out because you may find that one of them will go for such a great price that even if it's not your top pick the savings are more than worth enduring a minor disappointment.

If you do get yourself into an auto auction, the best thing to do is to go as a spectator the first time around. Look around closely, get a feel for how the whole process works. Once you feel confident in your abilities to discern what is going on, go back again as a potential buyer.

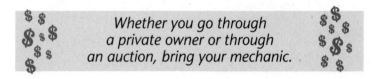

Whether you go through a private owner or through an auction, bring your mechanic.

By far the biggest worry associated with the used-car shopping experience is that you may find yourself owning a car that hasn't much life left in it. Although those worries have abated somewhat in recent years due to the surging market in high quality, late-model cars, they haven't gone away entirely. If you buy a used car from a professional dealership that offers a terrific warranty, you have some measure of peace of mind, but what if you buy from a private owner or an auto auction? Well, you'll be on your own. It's that simple.

In order to bring some measure of assurance to the process, the strategy to follow is to bring one's own mechanic to the point of sale so that he can give the car a thorough check (or as thorough as possible) of his own. It's best if you can bring a mechanic with whom you've already established an on-going relationship, but if you don't have one like that, there are mechanics who specialize in providing these kinds of services to prospective used car buyers. It may cost you $100 or so to have a mechanic do this for you, but it is probably the best $100 you'll ever spend. I realize that arranging with a mechanic to meet you for a prepurchase inspection can be a hassle, but do it anyway. Sometimes you can take the vehicle you're interested in to your mechanic's garage.

You can't shop with confidence unless you know the car's wholesale value.

When I was speaking about how to get a good deal on a new car, I said that the most important piece of information you need in hand is the invoice price of the car. Without that, it's really difficult to know where on the price spectrum a good deal really lies. Well, in the pursuit of used cars, it is the wholesale price that you'll want to know before you begin hunting. The wholesale price is the preowned car version of the invoice price; it tells you what the car is worth. With this information in hand, you can then tell if the selling price is really fair or not.

One thing to remember is that you won't have as much flexibility in prices as you would with a new car. New car dealerships will have substantially the same inventory, so there will be lots of versions of the same car available. The story is much different with used cars. Even if you find two cars that are similar in year, make, and model, each of those cars will have their own unique history that will alter the value. However, it is still essential for you to have the wholesale value information so you can know what the car is worth and what you're willing to pay for it.

Where do you go to obtain wholesale prices for used cars? In the new car section of this chapter I referred to a series of excellent buying guides known as the *Edmund's* series of guides. These reference materials are excellent, probably among the very best buying guides around. Well, as fortune would have it, *Edmund's* publishes guides on used vehicles as well. The information is just as comprehensive as that found in the new car guides. To get your hands on what you need from *Edmund's*, just make a trip to your local bookstore's "Reference" or "Automotive" section and take it from there. (You can also check them out on the Internet at www.Edmunds.com.)

Another excellent source is the *N.A.D.A. Official Used Car Guide.* This is a small, paperback book (really more of a thick booklet) with a bright yellow cover that is among the most official resources for determining what a used car is worth. There are all kinds of helps in the book, including demonstrations on how to adjust the car's wholesale value on the basis of what options it contains, as well as on the basis of high and low mileage. The book is very inexpensive and can be found at your local bookstore.

Leasing

These days, leasing has become the choice for many people looking to get into a new car. The biggest advantage to leasing is that you're not buying the car so you get the advantage of significantly lower monthly payments, which means you could be driving a luxury car for the purchase payments you would make if you had opted to buy a more practical vehicle. To that end, leasing is also attractive to many because the down payment requirements are very minimal. You have to part with a substantial up-front payment in order to get the car you really want to drive.

The problem with leasing is that too many people think they are saving money. Experts will tell you that leasing actually costs more in the long run. First of all, leasing is renting, which means you own nothing. When the lease term expires, all that you have to show for the period of time you drove the car, besides the satisfaction you've been deriving, is a bank account that is lighter because of the monthly lease payments you've been making. Even though cars depreciate significantly in value, once those purchase payments are done being made, you do own something of some measure of value. And if you've been caring for your vehicle properly, the residual value, while probably not great, may not be insignificant, either.

The biggest expense to leasing, besides the lease payments themselves, is the totality of the collateral costs that build up along the way. First of all, because you are renting you are obligated to return the car at the conclusion of the lease term in the same condition it was in when you first drove it off the dealership lot. This means you are on the hook for any damage to the vehicle—no matter how small it may seem to you. You know those little dings that every car seems to get from time to time, no matter how careful you are? You will be expected to pay for their repair. Also, leasing costs big because of the mileage limitations. Your standard lease agreement will cover only a certain number of miles per year. If you drive significantly more than the established limit, those miles will cost you a lot at turn-in time.

Overall, I would have to say that the decision as to whether or not a lease is good for you comes down to this: Are you the kind of person who feels that a car payment is simply a part of life like a home mortgage payment? If so, then leasing is probably the option for you. If, however, you are not one who is resigned to making a car payment every month, and in fact have no problem driving the same car many, many years after its model year, then leasing is definitely *not* for you. Someone with that mind-set will be much better off buying their vehicle, paying it off, and then enjoying the many payment-free months that will follow.

If you have decided that leasing is the better option for you, then it would behoove you to find as many ways as possible to save money on the whole venture. Here are some tips to help you cut the total leasing costs dramatically.

 Lease the same kind of car you would have purchased.

One of the biggest attractions of leasing is that the potential lessee can acquire a better vehicle for the same amount of monthly payment that he would make to purchase a less-noteworthy automobile. That's great, but if it is the simplicity of the turn-in of a lease vehicle, along with the simple desire to always drive a new-model car, that attracts you to leasing, then stick with leasing the same vehicle you would have otherwise purchased.

Opting to lease the more-expensive car is like the person who feels he is "saving" at the grocery store by purchasing an item he would not have otherwise purchased without a coupon. If he didn't have the 25-cent coupon in hand, he probably wouldn't have bought the additional $2 item.

Leasing does give you the opportunity to drive a more expensive car for a lower payment, but if you really want to save, drive the car you would have driven to begin with.

 Negotiate the cost of the vehicle before you agree to the lease.

When it comes to leasing, car dealerships like to give the impression that the costs of the vehicle to be leased are non-negotiable—that because you're renting, the rules are different and you must pay the sticker prices with no questions asked. *Wrong!*

Cars to be leased are every bit as viable for receiving a negotiated-down price as a car to be purchased. Unfortunately, few people will tell you that. The best way to accomplish your goal of negotiating down the cost of the car is to make your preparations in the same way you would if you were planning to purchase the car outright. Walk into the dealership with the invoice price of the car firmly in your mind and begin to bargain down the price of the car.

 Secure a shorter lease term.

I know that the attraction of lower payments causes many people to sign lease agreements that can last as long as five years. But if one of the main reasons a person is leasing is to be able to drive a new-model vehicle, why agree to a lease that means driving the same car for five years?

Keep your lease agreements short. This will help preserve the value of leasing, which is a main reason you chose it over buying in the first place. It is not unusual to find programs where payments are actually lower for short-term leases than they are for long-term leases because, from time to time, manufacturers who want to encourage increased driving of their products will introduce terms that actually save you money.

You should be advised that if you are hammering out an agreement for a longer-term lease and raise these concerns with the salesperson, he will likely tell you that it will be possible for you to break the lease whenever you want, and he'll help you lease another new car when you're ready to do it. Well, it may be possible to break the lease, but it is also quite certain that you will pay a substantial fee to do so. If the salesperson doesn't say anything about that, you may want to read your lease contract very carefully before you sign (which you should do anyway) to see if such a stipulation is present.

 Purchase extra miles in advance.

Standard lease agreements contain strict mileage limitations. In general, one cannot drive over 15,000 miles per year without having to buy additional miles at roughly 10 cents per mile. If you drive 20,000 to 30,000 miles per year (figures which are not at all unheard of), you may add to your leasing costs to the tune of $500 to $1,500 annually. For a three-year lease, you're looking at an additional expense at turn-in time of $1,500 and up to $4,500.

To keep these costs down, do a solid estimate of how many miles per year you think you will drive; overestimate, if you think you should. Give yourself an accurate picture of how much driving you'll be doing in your lease vehicle for each year you'll have it. Then, if you discover that the average annual figure exceeds the standard mileage limitation contained in the lease agreement, tell the salesperson you want to buy those extra miles up-front. Buying the extra miles this way will still cost you more money, but not nearly as much as it would if you waited to pay for them at the lease's conclusion.

Insurance

The purchasing of a car can represent a substantial investment, to be sure, but it is by no means the beginning and end of your car-related expenses. There are the costs associated with maintaining the vehicle (I'll talk a bit more about that a little later), and there is the often-pricey expense of insuring the vehicle for proper and safe use on the roadways of America.

Insurance is often expensive no matter what you are specifically insuring—life, limb, car, house, and so on. In this section, we're going to spend some time discussing car insurance . . . and how to save copious sums of money.

Make no mistake about it: Auto insurance is expensive. Nevertheless, there are many ways you can save a bundle on your overall costs; you just have to know what to do. In this section, I'm going to help you enjoy tremendous savings on your auto insurance. Best of all, none of the strategies are complicated to follow or implement. Their success is ultimately dependent on your willingness to incorporate them into your plans as you seek to stretch your consumer dollars.

 Raise your deductible.

By raising the deductible on your auto policy from $250 to $500, you can save roughly 25 percent on the annual cost of your premiums; by raising it from $500 to $1,000, you can knock off another 25 percent or so. Granted, once you raise the deductible, you are responsible for making up the difference out of pocket, but that's really not so bad. Let's say you currently have a $250 deductible, as so many of us have. You don't want to run to the insurance company every time you have a claim of at least $250 because, if you do, it may not be too long before your rates are raised significantly or your policy is canceled altogether. Keep enough money set aside in an emergency fund so you can pay for any damages to your car(s) that cost between $1 and $500. If you suffer damages beyond $500, then you can go to your insurance carrier for financial assistance. Without question, raising your deductible is the easiest step you can take to save a significant amount of money on your auto insurance.

 "Shop out" your coverage at least once a year.

One of the most common adages in the world of consumerism is the idea that if you want to get a good deal on something, shop around. As trite as it may be, it's very true—and in no other area of financial consumerism is it any truer than in the area of car insurance.

The disparity in insurance rates that exists from company to company can be ridiculous. It is not unusual to find the same coverage for the same family that differs in rate by as much as 50 percent, depending on the company providing the coverage. Typically, the variances are usually around 30 percent, but they can be greater. Still, a differential of 15 or 20 percent can mean a lot of money kept in your pocket because some auto policies for families can cost thousands of dollars in annual premiums. There are a huge number of factors that go into determining what a prospective insured's rates should be, and so it's hardly unusual that one company may process that information to come up with a rate result that is substantially different than that of another company.

The best way to determine if you are getting the best deal you possibly can is to comparison shop your policy with at least five different carriers once a year.

Dump your collision coverage once your car's value drops below $2,000.

Collision is the part of your auto policy that reimburses you for the costs associated with repairing your own automobile if it is damaged in an accident. When you buy a car through a lender, you will be required to maintain collision coverage on the car for the duration of the loan. The truth is, even if you paid for the entire car up front, you would still want to maintain collision coverage since the cost of fixing even a minor amount of damage can be expensive. Collision, then, is going to be a wise coverage for you to keep on a newer vehicle, even if it is not required by law in your state.

What should you do, though, when the value of your vehicle drops substantially over the years? At that point, do a general analysis of how cost-effective it is for you to maintain collision coverage. Remember, no matter how expensive the damage to your car might be, the insurer will never give you more than the car is worth. This means that if you sustain damage to your car in the amount of $2,500 and your car itself is worth $1,500, then the insurance company will "total" your car and pay you the $1,500. On top of this, collision coverage can be very expensive to maintain, and, unfortunately, its cost does not drop significantly as your car's value diminishes through the years.

Your strategy, then, should be to consider dumping your collision coverage once the value of your car drops below $2,000. At that point, the coverage starts to become unreasonably expensive in relation to the value of the vehicle. Sure, you'll be on the hook to finance the repair of the car if you sustain any damage, but assuming you've dropped the coverage and realized a savings, you can put that savings toward a new vehicle and not even bother repairing your old car.

Consider dropping your comprehensive coverage.

The same issues that arise with collision coverage arise as well with comprehensive. Comprehensive will reimburse you for damage sustained by your vehicle when the cause of the damage is something other than a collision, such as damage from weather and theft. Damage is damage and you face the same cost issues as you do with collision. If your car is worth less than $2,000, you may be unreasonably maintaining an expensive part of your overall insurance coverage. Once again, decide if you really want to keep your comprehensive coverage in the same way that you determined the viability of maintaining your collision insurance. I think you'll find that once your car drops below the $2,000 mark, you'll be better off pocketing the savings and putting it toward a new car.

Save money with an umbrella liability policy.

Another way to save significantly on your auto insurance is to become a little clever about how you insure for liability. An "umbrella" liability policy is one that offers comprehensive liability coverage on both your auto and home for a relatively small sum of money. In fact, $1 million of umbrella liability coverage should cost no more than $150 to $200 per year. Your strategy, then, should be to insure your cars and home for the lowest liability limits permitted by law, and then pick up the umbrella coverage as a way to cheaply cover the difference. Be advised, though, that you will not be able to obtain umbrella coverage unless you have both your home and auto with the same insurer (which is better, anyway, as most insurers give you a discount on both your homeowners and auto policies when you insure both through them). Also, you should make sure that you have not reduced your liability coverages on your individual home and auto policies until you know that your umbrella policy is in force.

Maintenance

As with so many other different kinds of goods purchased by consumers, lots of emphasis is placed on how to save money at the actual point of purchase, but not nearly as much attention is paid to the care and maintenance of those same goods. This can be especially significant when it comes to cars. There is really no other kind of high-dollar item one can purchase where the amount of care required to keep it running smoothly is so small in relation to its overall price. While I am no mechanic, to be sure, let's take this opportunity to touch on some basic services you can provide for your car to ensure that it will continue to run well for many years. Performing even the most minimal kinds of automobile services can save you thousands of dollars over the course of the life of your car, especially if you're someone who likes to hold on to cars for a long time and dreads the thought of spending money to buy a new one. Let's take a look at some things we all can do to greatly extend the lives of our automobiles.

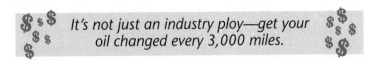

It's not just an industry ploy—get your oil changed every 3,000 miles.

We've probably all heard how important it is to change the oil in our cars every 3,000 miles, but many people look at that as being simply an industry ploy designed to keep consumers coming back for oil changes more often than needed. Oil is in many ways the lifeblood of the car, providing valuable protection to the engine and other important parts. As time goes on and you drive the car more and more, the oil will deteriorate and begin to dissipate. This change in viscosity reduces the valuable protection oil offers and doesn't allow the oil to cling to the engine's parts and to keep them well lubricated and running smoothly. Your entire engine, and all of its many moving parts, lives at the mercy of your engine oil.

Changing the oil is especially important if you drive in parts of the country where temperatures can be extreme. Even if you live in more moderate climates, you still need to change your oil every 3,000 miles or so. Changing the oil is a simple task that you can do on your own. Check out your library or ask your mechanic how to do the job. Remember, though, that your oil and oil filter should always be changed together.

*When you change your oil,
use a quality filter.*

Whether you change the oil on your own or have it done for you, remember: All oil filters are *not* created equally. Very few of us really put much thought into what kind of oil filters we are using, but it does make a difference. Cheap oil filters may not do nearly as good a job of filtering the oil, which exposes the engine to contaminants that can damage it over time. This can especially be an issue if you have your oil changed at one of the convenient "quickie" oil change operations that have sprung up all over in recent years. If they are not using a quality, name-brand filter (and you should always ask), then insist that they use one. If they don't carry them, buy your own and bring it with you so they can install it. (This should decrease the cost of the oil change, too.) Having your oil changed frequently will lose its value considerably if you are allowing a substandard oil filter to be used.

Pay close attention to the maintenance of your tires.

How often have we heard how important it is to keep the tires rotated and balanced? As with the changing of the oil, that task is something that's not done nearly as often as it should be. A quality set of new tires can run as high as $500, and that's a figure you'll be paying a lot more often than you should if you don't rotate and balance your tires. The wear on your tires must be mitigated as much as possible with proper maintenance to make sure that you don't have to replace them more often than absolutely necessary. Also make sure your car is properly aligned because that affects the wear pattern on your tires.

Whenever you buy your tires, make sure you are given free lifetime rotation and balance services on them. There are too many tire dealers out there who offer these services for free to pay extra for them anywhere else.

 Keep your engine running smoothly with quality air filters.

A little bit ago I discussed the importance of using quality oil filters in your car. The same principle applies to the air filter, as well. A quality air filter costs more, but for the protection it provides, the money you spend the money is well worth it.

One way you can feel better about spending that much on an air filter is to take steps to ensure that it lasts much longer than it might otherwise. Each month, remove your air filter and clean it: first by simply tapping it against the driveway so that the dirty particles are loosened, then by running water through it so that the filter is cleaned thoroughly. This is but another example of how taking an extraordinarily small amount of time and effort can help to save you big bucks throughout the duration of your ownership of your vehicles.

7

Investment Strategies

I have always been fascinated by the world of investing. I guess that explains why I became a stockbroker at the age of 21 and why I was one of the youngest people ever listed in *Who's Who in Business and Finance*. I love watching the markets and helping clients make money through their stocks and mutual funds. I know running charts and graphs all day and making pit-of-the-stomach buy-and-sell decisions is not a trip to Disneyland for everyone. But we all must become investors regardless of how much we enjoy or dislike the process. Other than working at our regular daily jobs, there is really only one other viable way we have to secure our long-term financial goals and dreams: investing. And today working a regular job isn't always enough to pay all of our living expenses and still have enough money left over to finance college educations, retirement, and a host of other goals long-term goals.

This chapter, however, isn't on the benefits of investing. The assumption I'm going to make is that you are already sold on investing and are looking for a way to save a lot of money doing it. In this age of increased consumer awareness, the days of being stuck investing through a full-service, full-price retail brokerage house are long gone. However, in order for you to realize a substantial financial benefit from all of the new, cost-effective ways there are to invest, you have to engage in some do-it-yourself activities, chiefly self-education.

I'm going to make a bold statement, but when you are done reading this chapter, I think you'll understand why I feel very comfortable making it: *I believe that full-service retail brokerage houses like Merrill Lynch and Paine Webber are obsolete for investors.* Some of you may be aghast that anyone could make such a statement, but the fact remains that it's completely true. There is absolutely no reason why you should have to pay the large commissions these firms charge just so you can have an opportunity to make your money grow. Your goal from here on out should be to invest as capably as you can and put as much commission money as possible back into your pocket. It can be done . . . and I'm going to show you how.

 Full-service retail brokerages are not your only option.

There is no question that, over time, the stock market will be your best opportunity for long-term investment success. Since the turn of the century, the stock market has returned to investors an average annualized return of roughly 10 percent, a rate that outpaces all other considered investment options. Unfortunately, the stock market has traditionally also represented one of the *priciest* investment from the standpoint of cost. Traditionally, securities investing was done through full-service retail brokerage houses, and these operations would normally charge the highest commissions allowed by law to place trades for you. Even though there have been alternatives to these full-service operations for a long while now, many people have resisted giving up their use out of deference to the perpetuated myth that only the experts can invest effectively on your behalf.

Don't believe it. There are many wonderful ways for you to invest for low—or even no—commission. The caveat is that you must be willing to expend some effort. *You* can learn about any of a number of excellent investment opportunities on your own and, in fact, make the trades on your own. You just have to get out there and do it. There are a great number of excellent resources to which you can refer to learn more about investing. There are a lot of mutual funds that you can invest in for no cost, and there are even individual stocks that you can invest for no commission! Sound amazing? Well, perhaps, but the real point is that *it can be done*. Would you like to know the secret? It's really not that difficult at all.

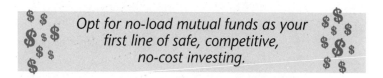

Opt for no-load mutual funds as your first line of safe, competitive, no-cost investing.

Mutual funds represent, by far, the best mix of safe investing, quality investing, and cost-effective investing. In my opinion, no other investment option comes close. With mutual funds it's possible to earn, over the course of many years, an average annualized rate of return of 12 to 15 percent—and many mutual fund investors have done better than that. Impossible, you say? Not at all. Before we discuss that particular point any further, however, let's take a peek at what a mutual fund really is.

Mutual funds are defined as companies that invest in individual securities with the intent of making a profit. So when you invest in a mutual fund, you are actually investing in the underlying portfolio of securities that makes up the fund. Mutual funds are managed investments, and the managers are usually compensated by receiving a percentage of the assets under management. The better the fund performs, the more money the manager or management team makes. Managers, however, are usually retained by short-term contracts, so if a particular fund is not performing well the company can quickly change the investment procedures and policies.

Mutual funds are considered very consumer-friendly for a variety of reasons. First, mutual funds are well diversified. A broad-based stock mutual fund may, for example, have as many as 100 different companies retained within its portfolio at all times, and that number can even be much, much higher. This diversification enhances the safety of stock market investing because it means your invested dollars are not riding on the fortunes of only one or two companies.

Additionally, mutual funds are popular because of the professional management that goes along with them. Because of this management, lay investors (and even those who are well-versed in these things) can sit back and rest assured that someone or some group who spends most of their time watching investments will be making the trades on their behalf. That is a great weight that many who have little knowledge about investing are happy to transfer to the shoulders of more experienced investors. It is this professional management of funds that has helped make full-service brokerages obsolete. After all, if you have money invested in a mutual fund, why do you need to retain an "account manager" at a brokerage firm?

Finally, mutual funds give smaller investors a fair crack at the big time. One of the long-held criticisms of the stock market is that it has traditionally been inaccessible to small investors. Mutual funds have changed that. Because they are essentially investments where client funds are pooled in order to purchase the underlying portfolio of securities, it is not necessary for any one investor to have a lot of money to get in. In fact, there are mutual funds out there that allow you to invest for as little as $250, and some with slightly higher minimums that will waive that minimum as long as you agree to invest as little as $50 per month.

It's easy to see why mutual funds are so very popular these days and why they have changed the investment landscape forever.

From the standpoint of commission structure, mutual funds come in essentially two styles: load and no-load. Load mutual funds are those that charge a commission to invest; no-loads do not charge any commission. There is no reason why an investor should agree to place his money in a load fund and give up 5 percent of his investment dollars as a commission when he can stick with a no-load and have all of his investment monies go to work for him buying fund shares. Unfortunately, load fund companies, some of which are the aforementioned full-service, retail brokerages, have done a good job misleading prospective investors into believing that paying the load actually provides them with value. It doesn't. The load fund is a dinosaur leftover from the days before increased consumer awareness gained a foothold in the investment industry. Here's an important point regarding loads: *There has never been any proof whatsoever that the paying of a load enhances investment return.* If you look at the list of top-performing mutual funds for a given period, you will find that there is a fairly equal representation of load and no-load funds. While I can't very well claim that there are not load funds that perform well, the evidence still suggests that you in no way must invest in one in order to realize great results from your investments.

The bottom line: *Consider only no-load mutual funds for your first line of investment.* If you need some help finding an appropriate no-load fund and/or fund family on which to focus your efforts, please refer to appendix C, "No-Load Mutual Funds."

 Buy your no-loads through a discount broker.

Traditionally, mutual fund investors have had to purchase their funds directly from the fund company. This created great inconvenience for investors who want to hold a portfolio of funds from a variety of fund companies. In the past, their only option was to set up different accounts at different fund companies, or families, and keep track of their selections using all the different statements and trade confirmations that would arrive in the mail for *each* individual fund. Needless to say, many investors quickly grew exasperated at the huge amount of paperwork they had to keep in order to maintain their records. One solution was for investors to "intradiversify" their holdings within the same fund family, but many people wanted to be able to hold different no-loads with different families with greater ease.

Enter the discount brokerages. In an effort to help shore up their client base, discount brokerages (sleeker, more cost-efficient alternatives to traditional brokerages) came out with programs designed to deal with this problem. Charles Schwab and Company, for example, has an excellent program whereby you can choose to invest in any of hundreds of no-load mutual funds from a wide variety of no-load fund companies for no transaction fee. What's more, you can invest in any number of these funds simultaneously, and you receive one monthly statement that covers the previous month's activities involving each fund.

Schwab and Company is not the only discount brokerage that makes such a service available. Others do it as well and are generally differentiated by their policies on minimum hold periods, transaction costs, and so on. While following this strategy doesn't directly put a substantial amount of money back into your pocket, it will save you a great deal of money by reducing the amount of time you have to use to keep your books and records straight.

   Look to the discount brokerages
for all of your brokerage needs.

The nice thing about discount brokerages is that there's really nothing you can do through a full-commission retail outfit that you can't do through a discounter. There are some definite differences between the two, but there's really no substantive reason why you can't opt for the discounter every time out.

The biggest reason for choosing the discount option is clearly price. Commissions on individual securities trades are significantly lower at discounters than they are at full-service firms. Furthermore, discounters will make available no-load fund opportunities (which we just spoke about), where full-commission firms will not. Also, many collateral expenses associated with investing (annual IRA custodial fees, for example) are usually much cheaper (and even free) at the discount brokerages.

What *do* retail brokerages offer that discounters don't? Perhaps the most-ballyhooed advantage of going with a full-commission firm is that an investor, in exchange for paying the commission, is assigned an "account representative" whose job it is to "oversee" the account. Did you notice how I put those terms in quotes? There's a reason for that. "Account reps" are really just salespeople. They may have substantial knowledge about money and markets, but the real reason they are there is to make more money for themselves and their firm—which means to generate commissions from the sales of investment products. I remember being told once that full-service firms are good for those people who want to be able to talk to someone anytime they call. I nearly fell over when I heard that. It's really a myth that paying a commission, or a load on a mutual fund, entitles you to talk to an account rep about your portfolio anytime you want.

In general, account reps dislike spending much time talking about anything unless they're talking about making sales. If you make a habit of calling your assigned account rep at a full-commission firm just to talk about your account, you'll probably find that sooner or later he becomes tougher to get hold of. Why? Because talking doesn't generate commission revenue for him. He wants to make *sales*. Yes, you'll be told that you have access when you first come on board, but once you stop doing your part to make the cash register ring at your full-commission firm of choice, you'll find it difficult to get through to someone you can talk to.

Another touted advantage of full-service, full-commission firms is that they can give you access (read "sell") to investments that discounters can't always carry. Limited partnerships are an excellent example of this type of investment. Although some discounters will hold partnership assets, called units, for you, they really have no mechanism by which you can buy the partnerships directly through them. But that's no great loss. Limited partnerships are generally unsuitable for most investors and carry with them a high degree of risk. The kinds of investments you would not normally be able to access through a discounter are transactions the average investor would be better served to stay away from.

The last "advantage" of going with a major, full-service retail outfit is that you will have access to research reports and other information so you can make more-informed investment decisions. This *is* a nice thing to have; the problem is, by itself, it's not worth paying high commissions on your buy and sell transactions. Unless you're an avid, sophisticated investor, you probably don't need this information anyway. For that matter, even if you are, there are myriad ways to obtain what you need without going through a retail broker—including resources on the Internet.

My analysis of the usefulness of full-service, full-commission retail brokerages may seem harsh, but with the advent of no-load mutual funds and discount brokerages, the full-service outfits have become obsolete. Use them if you want to, but do so only if you are averse to helping yourself invest. If you are willing to expend even the most minimal amount of energy to invest on your own, you definitely don't need a full-service brokerage. Everything you truly need to invest can be found at the discounters. If you can't get it there, then you don't really need it.

Buy stocks for no commission.

The spirit of consumerism moves onward and upward. Did you know that it is now possible to purchase stocks for absolutely no commission? You read that correctly. The term that is coming into vogue to describe the kinds of stocks that can be purchased this way is "no-load," taken from the no-load mutual funds that have long served as the best overall mechanism for commission-free stock market investing.

The phenomenon of no-load stock investing is a fairly recent occurrence. For years, the closest thing to no-commission stock investing available was the dividend reinvestment plans in which many individual companies allowed investors to participate directly. To participate in a dividend reinvestment plan, or DRIP, an investor had to be an existing shareholder of the company in question. Assuming he already owned some shares of company X (which he would have purchased through a brokerage of some sort), he could then go straight to the company itself to purchase additional shares.

The beauty of this, of course, is that by going straight to the company, brokers and commissions are avoided altogether. As the name suggests, the primary mechanism for buying the additional shares involved the dividends that these stocks would pay out from time to time; the investor would simply arrange to have his dividends reinvested directly back into the company for no cost, and that was about as close to commission-free stock investing there was. Some of the companies that offered DRIPs even let investors purchase additional shares for cash, but they still had to have purchased their initial shares through a brokerage.

Well, DRIP programs are still alive and well. Hundreds of companies offer them, and smart stock investors who do not seek to trade terribly actively have been wise to look to the DRIPs as an excellent way to add shares to their portfolio base for no commission. But, there is a new and even better way to buy stocks for no commission—through no-load stocks.

No-load stocks are those that permit investors to buy *all* of their shares directly from the associated company, even their very first ones. This is an innovation that may make DRIPs a thing of the past in short order. What's more, no-load stocks even feature the kinds of investment goodies that heretofore had only been available from brokerages and mutual fund companies. For example, no-load stocks give their investors the opportunity to invest automatically, via electronic funds transfer from a bank account directly into the stock. Also, no-load stock companies even provide IRA custodial services to investors, which is something that even some investment professionals don't know.

You're probably wondering why you haven't heard much about these unique opportunities before now. The reason is the fact that the investment industry is one of the most highly regulated industries in the world. The Securities and Exchange Commission, the federal watchdog of the industry, specifically prohibits any meaningful marketing of these plans by the companies that administer them. Beyond that, the only way you might hear about no-load stocks is from investment professionals, and most of them work on a commission basis, and since there are no commissions generated from no-load stock transactions, they're not actively promoted.

The downside to no-load stock investing is the fact that the shares you purchase in this fashion are registered in your name. Now, that may surprise some of you because you probably thought you were the owner of the shares you buy through a broker. That's not exactly true. When you buy shares of stock through a broker, you are usually buying them in a way that registers them in what is called "street name." This means that the shares are registered in the name of the brokerage through which they're purchased. When you buy shares like this, the company whose stock you're purchasing has no record of you as an owner. For those of you who have purchased stock through a broker, whenever you receive literature about the company in which you've bought shares, have you noticed from where it's sent? It's not sent by that company, it comes to you through the brokerage.

There's really no great harm done when stocks are purchased in street name. In fact, there can be distinct advantages. For example, stocks maintained in street name at the brokerage might be transacted with much greater ease than if you were the registered owner. If you want to quickly sell ABC Company to purchase XYZ Company, you really cannot do it when the shares are registered to you personally. Also, the custodianship of the shares by the brokerage relieves you of much of the administrative hassles associated with stock ownership. Last, because the physical shares are maintained by the brokerage, an entity well equipped to deal with the secure maintenance and tracking of certificates, there is minimal risk that they will be lost or stolen, risks that are ever-present when you maintain stock certificates on your property.

Fortunately, no-load stock companies have been able to anticipate and deal with the last problem. When you buy shares of a no-load stock, the shares themselves are recorded in what is known as book-entry form, which means that the ownership is officially recorded but you don't receive actual certificates. If an investor wants to retain possession of the certificate, he need only contact the company administering the plan, and a certificate will be created and sent out. Again, though, this is unwise. I would suggest that, if you do decide to go the no-load stock route, you stick with letting the company keep your shares annotated in book-entry form. If you have ever had to go through the hoop jumping required to replace lost or damaged certificates, you'll know what I mean.

I have not discussed the wisdom of including individual stocks in your investment portfolio. There is a lot of wisdom in the notion that relatively inexperienced investors are better off sticking with mutual funds. However, this chapter is not meant to be a discussion of investment strategies, suitability, or anything else related to issues other than the saving of money in the pursuit of a quality investment portfolio. If you know you want to go with stocks as part of your investment portfolio, and you're not looking to do a lot of trading that would make accumulating a portfolio solely of no-load stocks unwise, then the no-commission—or no-load—stock option is probably for you.

I invite you to refer to appendix C that lists many of the no-load stocks available. I chose to include only those stocks that permit investment by residents in at least 47 states. I trust you will find this information helpful. No-load stock investing is, without a doubt, the best recent innovation in dirt-cheap securities investing.

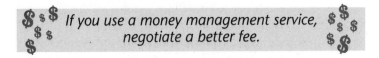

If you use a money management service, negotiate a better fee.

Many people in this day and age like to have a professional watching their investments for them. "Do-it-yourself investing is nice," they say, "but I feel more comfortable having an expert calling the shots." This can be especially true with folks who have large portfolios and feel the raw size is too large for them to effectively manage on their own. When they arrive at that conclusion, they look to a full-time money manager.

Without getting into a protracted discussion of the particulars of money managers, I do want to raise an important issue. As a full-time money manager myself, I want you to know you should *always* consider the possibility of negotiating the standard fee charged (assuming you have a large portfolio that gives you some leverage).

It's not likely that a money manager is going to give you a break on his standard fee if you come to the table with an amount of money that is close to his minimum account requirement. He has chosen a standard fee so that it can be the rule as opposed to the exception. However, if you have a substantial portfolio, one that any manager would be eager to take on and guide on your behalf, then by all means do some comparison shopping. Find out what each money manager brings to the table as far as reputation and qualifications. After narrowing your list to at least two of the managers you're considering, ask each person what kind of a deal he will cut you in exchange for the privilege of managing your money. If you have a portfolio valued at $500,000, and one manager will charge you three percent per year of the assets under management, and the other will charge you two percent, then guess what? You've just put $5,000 *back* in your pocket that year by going with the two percent manager. Also, you should know that even if you don't have a large sum of money beyond the minimum, you may still want to ask about a discount. Money managers are usually small, personal operations, and if you catch the main man at the right time and under the right circumstances, he may feel like giving you a break.

One caveat: If you have the ability to do it, negotiate the amount of the fee. However, be wary of shopping money managers solely on the basis of price. You need to base your decision on a great number of other factors, too. In fact, if a money manager seems like he's going to charge too little, you might want to be concerned. If he was quick to gain your account by undercutting all of the competition, he may have put himself in a place where he's making relatively little to manage the size of account you placed with him. Once the satisfaction of having secured your account wears off and he realizes how little he's really making, he may be less than enthusiastic about the overall management of your account—and that may decrease your return in the end.

 Handle your own investment strategizing.

If you know anything about me, you probably know that my principal business is that of serving as a money manager to several hundred clients all across the country. It is fascinating work, and I'm fortunate to be able to wake up each morning and look forward to doing a job that I love. Having said all of that, why would I, a person who makes his living chiefly as a money manager, encourage people to forsake money managers altogether?

Well, I'm going to be very honest with you. I know human nature well, and I know that even though many people can learn how to manage money themselves, they still prefer to have someone do it for them. Plus, there may be instances when it is actually a smart move to retain a money manager. Many people who have sizable portfolios but very little experience investing are probably good candidates for a professional money manager. However, if you have a portfolio that is of such a size you feel confident in your own abilities to manage it, then you may want to take the next step of learning professional money management techniques and applying them to your own investments.

Unfortunately, the scope of this book doesn't allow for an in-depth look at money management strategies because such a discussion could easily fill a book on its own. There have been many books written on investment management techniques through the years, and you can find periodicals on the subject at most newsstands. However, it *is* possible to learn the basics of real money management techniques and to implement these techniques in your own portfolio. All it takes is some explanation and an investment of time on your own. Let's get started.

Basic money management techniques can be categorized in two ways: *fundamental analysis* and *technical analysis*. Let's take a close look at each type, so that you can get a solid handle on how each one works.

Fundamental Analysis

Fundamental analysis involves the trading of stocks and mutual funds on the basis of the financial data that is specific to said stocks and funds. Analysts who subscribe to this type of money management are concerned with a company's earnings, its sales, its debt load, what kind of products it makes or services it provides, and a host of other specific pieces of financial information that are unique to the company itself. It is much more common to see this kind of analysis used in conjunction with individual stocks, as opposed to mutual funds; nevertheless, fundamental analysis can be used very effectively on mutual funds because some of the types of data that fundamentalists use when examining individual companies are available on behalf of funds, as well. Furthermore, fundamental data is defined a little differently between stocks and funds. For example, the list of companies in a mutual fund's underlying portfolio would be considered, by itself, fundamental information with respect to that fund. Helping the fundamentalist's cause on behalf of funds is the fact that fund reporting requirements have become more stringent in recent years, meaning there is much more information readily available about the fund's internal financial data measurements.

Overall, perhaps the most important piece of information that a fundamentalist will look at when considering an investment is the price-to-earnings (p/e) ratio. The p/e ratio is used to determine a stock's future prospects. If a p/e ratio is high, that means the current price is much higher than its level of earnings, which suggests that investors are willing to pay a premium for a stock that they believe will rise in value relatively soon. To fundamentalists, though, high p/e ratios can be a sign that a company is overvalued; if the earnings levels are that much lower than the associated stock price, there's a lot of room for the stock price to fall if the optimistic earnings predictions don't bear fruit.

On the other hand, a low p/e ratio suggests that there's more life in the company than the investors are willing to recognize. Fundamentalists pay close attention to investments with low p/e ratios because they may be general indications of a stock or mutual fund that is undervalued—and thus might move well in the near future. P/e ratios, however, cannot be evaluated on their own; they must be evaluated in conjunction with other fundamental data. A low p/e ratio, for instance, is not necessarily an indicator of a good investment play. The p/e may indeed be low because investors are right not to have a lot of confidence in that company's future prospects.

Speaking generally, p/e ratios of 20 or more are considered high, while p/e ratios of 10 and under are considered low. P/e ratios between those two figures are considered neither specifically high or low and can be taken to mean that investors are expecting an average level of growth in the near-term future.

One more thing about p/e ratios: Although some try to get mileage from doing it, it really is not appropriate to compare p/e ratios of companies from different industries. Comparing p/e ratios in that way is definitely a case of comparing apples and oranges. The figures are just not relevant that way. The p/e of a company that makes bicycles is not going to tell you much if you're comparing it to that of a utility company.

There is much more to fundamental analysis than just looking at the p/e ratio, however. You also need to pay close attention to a company's record of sales. If sales seem to be increasing that may be a sign that the company's base is strengthening and will continue to be profitable for investors through dividends or reinvestments into the company to fund expansion and growth—both good news. Also, a fundamentalist will want to look at the dividend activity exhibited by a particular investment. If you're looking at larger companies in your analysis, pay close attention to the direction of the investment's *dividend yield*. If the dividend yield of a company is showing signs of dropping, that may be a sign that the company is headed for problems. Remember, though, that many smaller companies are still in their primary growth stage and either pay dividends infrequently or not at all. So make sure you're considering the actual investment itself before you make a judgment on that basis. One excellent way to examine dividend yields is in a "macro" sense: examining the dividend yields of indices as a whole, like the Dow Jones Industrial Average (DJIA). If the dividend yield of indices like the DJIA and S&P 500 are at five percent or greater that generally means that a down market has come to an end and it may be a good time to buy back into the market. If the dividend yields are at three percent or below, it may mean that an up, or "bull," market has just come to an end, which means that investors may be getting into an overvalued market.

The last indicator we'll look at in our discussion of fundamental analysis is that of interest rates. Although broad-market interest rates are certainly not direct pieces of company-specific financial data, they do produce an effect on investments everywhere. Higher interest rates suggest that it will cost more for companies to borrow, which will eat into profits. Lower rates suggest just the opposite. When you see the stock market have a terrible day after even *talk* of a hike in interest rates, now you know why. Investors will sell their positions, anticipating that company revenues will be adversely affected by the higher cost of borrowing.

If you want to incorporate fundamental analysis into your investment strategy, you need to get started with a few simple things. First, you will need a notebook so you can track the data you will now be checking. You'll also want to become familiar with papers like the *Wall Street Journal* and *Barron's*, which will contain several key pieces of fundamental data for you to examine. Also, you will want to read *Value Line* reports—one-page stock analysis reports available on just about every publicly traded company—which will contain a plethora of useful data. *Value Line* reports can be found in the business reference section of your local library.

Don't be in a hurry. Start by feeling your way around for a while and looking at different companies and the fundamental data of each. See how it goes. If you find you're getting the hang of it, then you may want to do all your investment management by yourself, on your own terms. First, though, read on so that you may discover the other broad type of money management: technical analysis.

Technical Analysis

Theoretically, true technical analysts couldn't care less about a company's fundamentals—not its sales, its earnings, its dividend yields, and so on. In fact, "technicians" don't even care what a company does (what it makes or what services it provides). Technical analysis is more external; it's about watching the *historical* price movement of an investment as a means of predicting *future* movement. Technicians use instruments such as charts and graphs to plot an investment's price activity.

Technical analysts differ from fundamentalists in that they believe, philosophically, that it is the overall activity of the market, and an investment's specific movement against that backdrop, that is more important than a company's internal financial data measurements. Technicians believe individual investments are ultimately at the mercy of the market, regardless of how solid a company's fundamentals look.

Technical analysis software packages exist in abundance, but you don't need a computer to incorporate technical analysis into your portfolio-watching efforts. As a matter of fact, one of the most historically revered methods of technical analysis, the *moving average*, can be implemented with nothing more than a pencil, a piece of graph paper, and a newspaper.

Moving averages represent the core of what technical analysis has become in recent years. The most basic definition of a moving average is that it is the running average of an investment over a set length of time. For example, a 200-day moving average is the average price of an investment calculated for a period of 200 days. The average "moves" because with each new day the oldest day's price is dropped from consideration and the average is then recalculated to come up with the most current average price.

To properly utilize a moving average in order to make investment decisions, you must compare it with the current price of the security you're analyzing. For example, if you are trying to make transactional decisions on ABC Fund, you would look at its current price and look at its moving average price. My advice is that you get some graph paper and chart two separate price activity trends: the price of the security's moving average and the security's current actual price. Use two different colored pencils to make your dots, so that it will be easy to tell whether a particular price represents an actual current price or a moving average price. (You may also want to connect the dots for additional clarity.)

As your chart is coming together, you can begin to use it to make buy and sell decisions. If a security's price crosses its moving average moving upward that is regarded by technicians as a buy signal; by contrast, if the price crosses its average moving downward that is considered a sell signal.

Of course, you can tailor your moving average analysis a number of ways. Perhaps the biggest decision you have to make is what length of moving average you want to maintain. The longer the selected moving average period is, the more conservative the results. A longer moving average period (a 25-week moving average) will mean you move less frequently. If the period is shorter (a 5-week average), you will move more frequently. I suggest you keep *two* moving averages going, one shorter in length and the other longer. That way you can compare both charts before making your decisions. Also, I suggest that you base your length terms in weeks, not days, when using mutual funds because these funds are priced only once per day, so their movement is not nearly as potentially volatile as is that of individual stocks. If you do opt to note the prices weekly, try to be consistent by getting your prices on the same day each week.

For example, a 5-week moving average is going to consist of the closing prices of a mutual fund taken once a week, on the same day each week, for the past five weeks. When the following week's price is added, the oldest one is discarded, and the average is recalculated. Use the same process for a longer term.

To get started, pick a few funds and start watching them just for kicks. To calculate your initial average, you will have to locate the previous weeks' or days' prices for the funds or stocks you've chosen to watch, going back as far as your chosen term length requires. One brief trip to the library should accomplish that. After you have the initial averages calculated, you will need only stay current with the new prices, and then recalculate your averages each day or week.

You may find that you prefer one method of analysis over another, but I recommend doing both. Either way, by becoming a master of at least the basics of one or both analysis types, you will be able to manage your investments more professionally, reducing your investment expense to no greater than the minimal time and effort required each day or week. *That is a bargain.*

8

Lowering
Higher Education Costs

One of the grandest dreams for parents is to be able to stand in an auditorium or college football stadium and see their children receive the "sheepskins" that signify they are college graduates. Not only is the goal of attaining a college degree one that fills parents and children alike with thoughts of pride and images of prestige, but it also carries with it some substantial real-world value. One of the trends now is for older adults to go back to school and get a degree. Studies have shown that individuals with bachelor's degrees will earn, on average, about $1,000,000 more over the course of their lifetimes than those who have only high school diplomas. There's no guarantee, of course; there are a lot of people who have low-paying jobs who are college graduates, and there are some high school graduates (even some high school dropouts) who have achieved tremendous business success. Nevertheless, if your child, or you, chooses to major in something that has a great deal of marketability associated with it, there is little question that he or she will have a big headstart in the income-chasing game.

A lot of information on what is known generically as "financial aid," such as loans and grants, can be found with ease at the college-advising center of any high school, so I want to focus on some less-frequently considered mechanisms to help make a college education more affordable. These strategies are unusual, but they are viable and worth investigating if you're serious about seeing your child, or you, earn a college degree without ending up in the poorhouse in the process.

Okay, enough idle chit-chat . . . let's get on with the business of lowering the cost of a college degree

Consider a distance-learning program.

In this day and age, there are many unconventional methods a person can use to obtain a college degree. One of these methods is "distance-learning." Distance-learning involves studying for a degree primarily at home, with materials obtained through the mail, via computer, or on TV. Purists sneer at what they call "mail-order degrees," but don't sell this method of getting an education too short. Although there are, admittedly, a lot of turkeys in the world of distance-learning, there are also some very fine programs available through major, regionally accredited universities that will stack up very nicely against degrees obtained for a lot more money and a lot more hassle.

This method of obtaining a degree is considered more ideal for older students who don't have the time to go back to school full-time in more traditional environments and who aren't interested in experiencing the stereotypical college existence. Nevertheless, this is a viable route for all who wish to earn a degree. The greatest benefit to obtaining a degree in this fashion is that the costs are much, much less than they would be even if you attended a public university as an in-state resident. It is possible to earn a viable, quality degree through a distance-learning program for as little as one-tenth the cost of a traditional degree program.

If you want to learn more about these programs and find out which ones are best throughout the country and the world, I strongly suggest you pick up a copy of *College Degrees by Mail* by Dr. John Bear, Ph.D. Dr. Bear is one of the world's foremost authorities on distance-learning programs, and his book is second-to-none in its handling of the subject. The book is updated regularly to provide readers with the most current information available. You may pick up a copy of *College Degrees by Mail* in the "reference" section of a bookstore or, if they don't have it, they can order it for you. You might get some mileage out of perusing a copy at the library, but remember that the information is somewhat time-sensitive: schools may change features of their programs, including that having to do with tuition. Also, because Dr. Bear is good about evaluating these programs on an on-going basis, you can be sure that the latest edition of this book will have the very best programs available to you.

 Consider attending night school.

College is by no means something that can only be attended during the day. There are many colleges that offer programs at night, and these will have some of the lowest tuition costs of any "on campus" or classroom programs available.

Night schools basically come in two types. The first type is the one that is the standard degree program of the local university which sponsors the classes. In other words, instead of attending classes at the university during the day, you attend the classes at night. Night school will typically offer some solid value to students, but be forewarned. If you're attending a program like this, then basically the only difference between day students and night students is the time of day classes are being attended. You will be less likely to realize a substantial savings on tuition this way.

The other option is to attend one of the satellite campuses of the many "chain" colleges that have sprouted up throughout the country. You may be familiar with some of these programs; it's not unusual to find these schools advertising on local television, encouraging working adults to consider them as a means of finishing their formal educations. Also, you may drive past their campuses from time to time, which are sometimes located in professional office buildings and even strip malls. Don't be too terribly put off by their locations. Even though you won't choke on the ivy if you attend schools like these, you or your child will be able to attain a quality education.

One thing to be aware of is that many of these programs specialize in business-oriented degrees, which means that if your dream is to study humanities, you may be out of luck. The idea is that working adults are most likely seeking business degrees that will help them advance professionally, so there is little call for a liberal arts program that will not fill that requirement directly. However, if a bachelor of arts or bachelor of science in business administration is what you're seeking, then these opportunities may be for you. The tuition costs of these programs are greatly reduced over those of traditional schools—sometimes as much as 50 percent—in large part because they don't have the overhead of traditional colleges and universities. If you want to find out more about what's available in your area, look in your phone book's Yellow Pages under "Schools—colleges and universities."

Reduce the amount of time
it takes to obtain a degree.

Regardless of what kind of college attended, there should always be ways available for motivated students to help speed up the process of getting the degrees they desire. First, there are the programs like AP (Advanced Placement) and CLEP (College Level Examination Program) that let students forego taking required courses if they are able to pass examinations in any of a variety of subject areas (a student is said to be able to "CLEP out" when he passes an exam that allows him to fill an academic course requirement). You should inquire of all "credit by experience" options that may be available to you, as well as whether or not it's possible to obtain credit for what is known as "life experience" (life-experience credit, however, is not going to be readily available to younger students for obvious reasons). The key to this method is to try as much as possible to get out of having to take the credit-hours that make college so expensive.

Another mechanism for obtaining a college degree more cheaply is to accelerate the rate at which college is attended. Greater value is realized, for example, when you take more courses in the same semester. Most students take only the minimum numbers of credit hours necessary to maintain full-time status; what's wrong with taking a few more each semester, having a little less free time on your hands, and wrapping up your degree a year to 18 months earlier? Granted, you will likely be paying by the credit hour for your degree, so there's no real savings there, but if you're living on campus, the cost of your residency declines if you're able to take more classes at the same time and ultimately graduate earlier. You'll also enter the workforce sooner, which means you're able to recoup your college costs quicker.

Attend a community college.

Many people take for granted the idea that they must spend all four years in pursuit of their bachelor's degrees at four-year schools. However, not only is that usually unnecessary, it also may be costing you big. The fact is, the work done in college during the first two years is essentially the same, regardless of where you go. Freshman and sophomore college years are spent primarily knocking out the required courses, or prerequisites, that allow you to move on and take the meatier upper-level courses that really account for your degree train-ing. The lower-level courses can be found at community colleges as much as they can be found at four-year schools, The difference, of course, is that community colleges, while maintaining high standards, usually have tuitions that are much less than four-year schools.

The community college option is viable; there's little question about that. However, before pursuing it with great confidence, you need to do some homework to make sure that the courses you take at a community college will be *transferable* to a four-year school. There are numerous stories of individuals who went to community colleges for the first two years of their bachelor's degree programs with the intention of saving money overall, only to find that not everything they took was transferable—and therefore had to be repeated, costing them and their families more money, not less, in the long run.

*Go to college part-time . . .
and work full- or part-time.*

The costs of college, along with so many of life's other little realities, are forcing families to rethink the way the college experience should play out. The days of the resident, four-year college experience are not as common for students as they once were. With annual increases in college costs outpacing the yearly rate of inflation by about four percent, there is more and more thought going into how a degree can be obtained without driving families into the soup line.

For many students the answer lies in formulating an acceptable combination of work and school. While most experts tell you that having the ability to concentrate on school full-time is most conducive to the learning process, many realists say that a happy medium has to be struck so that it's even possible for students to attend school. Working and attending school at the same time will add to the length of time it takes to garner that sheepskin, but there is a *big advantage* to this method of cutting costs: By the time the graduate enters the work-force full-time, he or she has already spent time working in the real world, which might provide an advantage over other graduates who only spent their college years attending classes.

The exact mixture of time spent working versus time spent going to school will vary with each student. Every person's capacity to handle a varied and full workload will differ, so thoughtful consideration should be put into just how the schedule should be composed. The important thing is to remember to make forward progress. If you allow yourself to become bogged down with work, it won't be long before your schoolwork suffers and you begin taking classes at an even slower rate—or stop taking them altogether. At that point, the value of this strategy is severely mitigated.

 Consider the military as a means to finance your college costs.

There are a lot of opportunities these days for young people to look to the military as a means of paying for school. In fact, one of the members of my staff did just that, and he raves about it still. Not only are there generous tuition-funding programs that are accessible through military service, but the added benefit of military service gives your resume a real plus.

Employers love to see young people who have spent time in the military; successful completion of an enlistment term or appointment as an officer suggests to employers that a prospective job candidate is a team player, able to work in difficult environments, oriented toward discipline and respect for chains of authority, and, of those who utilized their military involvement to obtain a degree, are willing to make a great sacrifice in pursuit of a college degree.

In a nutshell, military programs for education can be categorized in one of two ways: programs in which one goes to college *before* military service, and programs in which one goes to college *following* military service. With the former, I'm essentially speaking of officer-training programs, while the latter refers to enlisted personnel who may wish to attend college following discharge.

Perhaps the most accessible college funding option available to students who wish to attend school *first* is the Reserve Officers' Training Corps, or ROTC. Although a student may participate in ROTC during all four years in college, it is during the last two years that he will receive a monthly allowance that totals over $1,000 per year. However, for motivated students, there is the opportunity to obtain college scholarships through the ROTC program, as well. However, be forewarned that recipients of ROTC scholarships will be expected to make a commitment to serving in the branch of the military represented by their ROTC involvement for several years. Also, the scholarships are granted largely on the basis of academic achievement, so there is a great deal of competition that exists for them. Nonscholarship ROTC participants have service commitment, as well, but it is quite minimal; in fact, most nonscholarship ROTC graduates simply serve in the reserves for a couple of years.

In addition to ROTC options, prospective college students may wish to look to one of the country's elite U.S. service academies as a means of obtaining an outstanding college education. Institutions like West Point (U.S. Military Academy) and Annapolis (U.S. Naval Academy) are some of the most respected in the realm of higher education. Only those who are convinced they want a real career in the military, however, should pursue U.S. service academies. For one thing, the service commitment required following graduation is generally about five years. Additionally, the schools themselves are very different from typical colleges and universities. The military lifestyle begins from day one and doesn't stop until graduation. Freshman year can be especially trying for students, known usually as cadets or midshipmen, where acclimation to military life is compounded by the tremendous pressures applied by both upper-level students and staff to see if the new additions can really cut the mustard. The financial benefits of service academy attendance and graduation cannot be denied, however. Not only do students attend cost-free for all four years, but they are paid a small salary to boot. Additionally, the reputation of service academies is such that if graduates wish to exit military service after their commitment is up, they will usually find many companies who will pay a premium if the graduates will go to work for them. Clearly, though, service academy attendance is not for everyone. Only those most highly motivated toward a military career and who feel they are well suited to existing within the often-challenging military lifestyle should consider applying for appointments.

For those who might want to reverse the order in which they do the college and military two-step, each branch has its own college savings program. Some are much more generous than others, which I always thought was kind of curious given that it's all the same government (it's typically that way, though, out of deference to the differing manpower goals that must be met by each service). My experience is that the army has some of the best programs, giving enlistees the opportunity to earn as much as tens of thousands of dollars for college over various periods of enlistment. The longer the enlistment, the more money that's available. Also, many of these programs exist on behalf of reservists and National Guardsmen as well as for full-timers. That can be a nice route to take for the individual who likes the college-financing benefits the military has to offer, but who is not sure he or she would be happy serving as a full-time, active-duty military personnel.

The best way to learn more about the variety of programs available through the military is to visit a local recruiting station for more information. Be warned that when you walk in the recruiter will try to convince you to sign up right away, but if you let him know up front what your interests are, you should find that he or she will be most helpful. Additionally, although recruiting stations exist primarily to sign up enlistees, as opposed to officers, the recruiter will be able to assist you in learning more about college funding programs that are available to prospective officers as well.

 Stick with public colleges and universities.

Even though it may be your dream to send your child to Harvard or Yale, your budget may not allow for much more than the cost of attending the public university system in your state. Don't fret. There are many more second-rate private schools out there than there are Harvards and Yales, and experts in this area will tell you that you're actually much better off going to a public university with a solid reputation than to a private university that is not terribly noteworthy. Even if your public university doesn't have a grand, nationwide reputation, it really doesn't matter. It's best to attend college in the same general area where you plan on working, so if you are attending the local state university, you probably are going to have all the "reputation" you'll need to obtain a job somewhere in the general local area.

Public universities cost roughly half as much as private universities, but the savings can be much greater. Additionally, because public universities are supported primarily from the tax base, it is less likely that tuition will rise in any substantial way.

*Attend college close to home
and save by commuting.*

Tuition is not even close to being the sole expense for those students seeking the "typical" college existence. Room and board can take a huge chunk out of the family college budget. Therefore, if you will be attending college at an area school, consider seriously the idea of living at home instead of on campus. It has been estimated that some people can save as much as $5,000 to $7,000 per year by doing this. While, admittedly, you won't have as much fun living at home as you would in the dorms, that may not be such a bad thing, especially when you're a younger student just becoming familiar with college life and facing all of the opportunities and temptations that go along with it.

*Find a school that specializes in
co-operative education.*

"Co-ops" are schools that are specifically set up so that students will have to work in addition to attending classes. However, these schools don't exist simply to help students pay for their own schooling, although that is clearly one main benefit. These schools also give students the opportunity to apply what they learn in the classroom to the workplace *before* they must face it full-time. It takes roughly five years for a student to complete a bachelor's degree if he participates in this kind of a program. Although the largest employer within the realm of cooperative education is the federal government, there are many private businesses out there that participate in cooperative education programs. Again, although the money one can earn for school through this type of program is clearly an attraction, I personally think the greater benefit is the fact that students can begin working in their chosen career while going to school, making themselves more attractive to prospective employers upon graduation. If you want to find out more about this wonderful way to obtain a college education very cost-efficiently, contact the National Commission for Cooperative Education, 360 Huntington Ave., Boston, MA 02115.

 Look into resident advisor opportunities at your school.

If you've ever been to college and lived on campus, you likely remember at least one of your resident advisors, or RAs. These were the people who helped the university departments of student affairs and housing keep the dorm ship running smoothly. RAs perform a variety of functions, including supervising organized study halls, settling problems between roommates and other residents, enforcing university rules in the dorms, and acting as a liaison between certain university departments and the residents. The job of an RA is quite important, so RAs receive nice breaks on tuition and/or room and board. However, in addition to the work, RAs are also required to spend a lot more time on campus, including rotating job schedules like weekend duty and attending all sorts of meetings. Before you apply to become an RA, talk to one or two of them to find out the *real* deal—and make sure it's something you really want. By the way, RA positions are usually only open to upperclassmen.

 Are you or your spouse an alumnus?

If you or your spouse is a college graduate, you may benefit from that college experience once again. Many colleges and universities have provisions whereby children of alumni will receive discounts on tuition. This is especially prevalent at smaller, private universities where revenue may be more difficult to come by. I suggest you contact the relevant universities early on to determine what kind of discounts might be available.

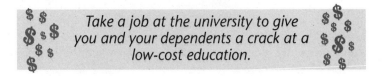

Take a job at the university to give you and your dependents a crack at a low-cost education.

This strategy is a little bold and it will take some daring and some commitment on your part. But, if your circumstances are right, it may be just the ticket for securing *low-cost* or *no-cost* college educations for you and your dependents.

You may already know that children of professors can attend the school for very little cost, and oftentimes no cost at all. Did you know, however, that the same tuition policy regularly applies to *all* employees of the university, whether or not they specifically work in academia? It doesn't matter if you work in the kitchen, for campus security, or as an administrator—you will enjoy generous tuition breaks that will usually include generous breaks for family members, as well.

Depending on your circumstances, you may want to consider changing jobs to help significantly lower the costs that will be incurred when your kids go to college. Obviously a great deal of planning needs to go into this strategy on the personal front. Additionally, you need to find out all of the "ins" and "outs" associated with getting a job at the university, especially as they pertain to the rules and regulations surrounding tuition discounts.

This is not just a strategy for parents. A sharp variation of this strategy would be for your children to get jobs on campus, for example in a security guard position. Not only would they be working, but they would likely receive full tuition reimbursement as employees of the university. If your kids are going to try and work their way through college, they might as well make life as easy on themselves as possible.

Some employers offer substantial tuition reimbursement opportunities.

If you happen to have a job with a large company, there's a good chance that you have, as one of your benefits, the opportunity to receive substantial reimbursements on your tuition *from* said company. Few people ever take advantage of these benefits, but if you don't have a college education and you *do* aspire to move up in the world, then you'd be foolish not to jump all over this. Companies make it available chiefly in the hopes that you will keep all of that new education you acquire in the company, that you will remain with the company as you continue your education, making the deal, from the company's perspective, less of a benefit to be paid out, and more of an investment. Obviously, this strategy is not terribly usable by young college students, as it is specifically designed for workers, and the plans rarely include reimbursement for dependents. Still, if you have tuition reimbursement available to you, I suggest taking it. It is one of the very best deals around.

A word in closing: I purposely stayed away from some of the common subjects normally found in discussions of college funding. I chose not to discuss grants and scholarships because most people know they exist, and the chances of the average college student getting one are really pretty slim despite some of the hype to the contrary. There are, indeed, a lot of scholarships available that year after year have no recipients; however, that's in large measure because many of them have unusual criteria so it's difficult to find anyone eligible.

As for loans, just about anything you need to know can be found through your child's high school counseling office, as well as through the financial aid department of any university or community college.

I also avoided discussing the financial planning approach to saving for a child's college education. The vast majority of people with whom I come in contact on this subject are already way behind on that approach. To be effective, one really needs to get started many years before the child or other designated person is ready to start school. To learn more about how to invest in order to fund a college education (as well as any other long-term goals), I would direct you to two previous books of mine, *More for Your Money,* and *Money Management for Those Who Don't Have Any,* both available at your local Christian bookstore.

My goal in this book was to try to help you explore and consider unusual avenues that will open up your options for education financing.

9

Reduce
Legal Expenses

I have to admit I am somewhat of a "legal junky." I watch all of the legal shows like "Rivera Live," "Burden of Proof," "Court TV," etc. I've had the opportunity to attend one year of law school as well. Despite my interest in law, I hate to pay a king's ransom for legal services. I've discovered that we can do on our own much of what lawyers will charge us thousands for.

Legal disputes are common, everyday occurrences that are, in fact, becoming *more* common by the minute. Huge jury awards through the years have given Americans the idea that if they've been wronged, especially by a large corporation, they might become instant millionaires. Even in cases of very minor disagreements, an apology and a promise to right the wrong is no longer enough. Today's philosophy is "keep your mouth shut until you get to your lawyer's office, and then the two of you can figure out how much in damages to sue for."

Can you tell I'm one of those in favor of some legal reform? I believe there should always be substantial civil redress available to people who have suffered significant and obvious physical and/or financial injury at the hands of another person or company who was clearly acting in a negligent or malicious fashion. However, there should also be mechanisms in place that force individuals who have suffered wholly or partially by their own negligence or outright stupidity to absorb whatever damages they may have suffered. Until that day comes, however, lawsuits will continue to abound.

In this hyperlitigious society, the person with little or no money must resolve to take matters into his own hands as much as possible. A person can successfully defend himself (or take the righteous offensive, as the case may be) and win without a lawyer, but he must be committed to the task at hand. Let me show you some ways you can negotiate unscathed through a maze of potential legal entanglements. I want to say right up front that I am not a lawyer. The following ideas, culled from years of living and working as a consumer advocate, are representatives of good (and perhaps clever!) common sense that is available to everyone, not just to those engaged in the formal study or practice of law. That being said, I do want to take this opportunity to advise you that the legal concepts illustrated and defined in this book are done so generally, and the assistance suggestions are not intended to be a substitute for specific legal advice from a competent legal professional.

It should also be noted that you would do well not to try and represent yourself in complex or challenging legal matters. For example, you'll notice that I have not included any helpful hints on how to best act in your own defense if you're charged with murder. As with most things, there's a point where it's best for laypeople to step back and let the professionals take over. However, if money is limited, that point, by necessity, may come later for you than it does for others.

Without further delay, then, let's take a look at 20 common legal conditions or situations that people may find themselves facing during the course of their lives.

Defend yourself against "abuse of process."

We have the right to sue someone in civil court for a variety of reasons. That's why courts exist, in part, to give the citizenry a means of seeking redress fairly and without violence. There are a number of ways in which the court system can be used to help individuals and groups seek damages and right wrongs that have been committed against them. People do not, however, have the right to use the court system in an effort to harass or intimidate others. If someone wants to sue a person for libel, for instance, and he is doing so because he honestly believes he's been libeled, fine. However, if he's suing that person for libel simply because he has an interest in seeing the other person spend copious amounts of money defending himself, that is not fine. Use of the court system in such an unscrupulous fashion is known as abuse of process.

Abuse of process occurs usually in the court system, but it can also be committed outside the strict arena of the courts. For example, if "Charlie" is angry with "Sam" over a personal matter and calls the police to falsely report that Sam is in possession of illegal drugs, Charlie has committed abuse of process if the complaint is investigated. Abuse of process can be a terrifying experience for people, but if you suspect that you are a victim there are ways to fight back that don't require a lawyer.

First, contact the clerk of the court in your community. The clerk of the court is the administration division of the court, and they will be able to access pertinent information regarding your case. Before you call have your thoughts in order and be able to explain clearly and concisely why you feel you're a victim of abuse of process. It will help if you take the time to write down all of the important points you want to mention to the person in the clerk's office. When you call, be sure to mention that you want to solve this problem without having to hire a lawyer. You'll likely receive some good advice about what to do in that regard.

Second, try to ascertain if the person you believe is committing the abuse of process hired an attorney to draw up any of the legal papers which have been used thus far. If so, contact the local bar association and make a formal complaint against that attorney.

Third, contact the Office of the Attorney General in your state and file a complaint with them as well, even though your purpose is to make the person who is initiating the abuse stop bothering you. By filing with the attorney general's office you are encouraging the start of an investigation into the activities of the person harassing you.

By following these three steps to their fullest conclusions, you will likely come to enjoy the remedy you are seeking.

Demand satisfaction
when your privacy has been invaded.

Invasion of privacy is a term we have all heard used formally and informally. In very general terms, invasion of privacy has to do with the rights people have to protect themselves from public scrutiny. Invasion of privacy has, over the years, evolved into a very complex area of civil law. As a result, there are now four generally accepted standards of privacy invasion that may be applied today when this subject arises. These are *intrusion, false light, private facts,* and *appropriation.* Let's take a closer look at each one so you will be able to more convincingly make your case if and when the need arises.

Intrusion invasion pertains to obvious and intentional interference into a person's personal privacy. In this case, the offending party can be held liable if he or she is guilty of an intrusion that would be regarded as highly offensive by an average member of society. When you read about celebrity photographers who dog their targets at every turn being sued for invading the privacy of those stars, it is the intrusion standard of this concept that is the basis for the suit.

False light invasion is defined as "publicity placing a person in a false light in a manner which would be highly offensive to a reasonable person of ordinary sensibilities." This type of invasion of privacy is typically invoked when the victim is embarrassed by a falsehood that is publicized. As an example, a clergyman who is a well-known member of the community could sue under the provision of the *false light* invasion of privacy standard if it is falsely reported in the media that he had been seen consorting with prostitutes. In order to win, though, he would have to prove that the newspaper either knew all along that the story wasn't true or that it acted with a reckless disregard for the truth.

Private facts invasion is interesting in that it allows a person to sue when someone has publicly reported a fact about him that is absolutely true (compare this to *false light* invasion of privacy)! The idea behind this is the protection of one's right to live his or her private life without scrutiny, no matter how unappealing society at large may view the facts about said private life. Thus, private facts invasion of privacy could just as accurately be referred to as *breach of trust* or *breach of confidence* invasion of privacy. For example, a patient could successfully sue a psychologist if he publicizes confidential information about that patient. A prospective plaintiff in a private facts invasion of privacy case must be able to satisfy two conditions: First, the publicity must be considered highly offensive by a reasonable person, and second, it must be shown that the information or facts which come to light by virtue of the publicity do not serve the public interest. If those two tests are satisfied, he has a case.

The final standard of invasion of privacy is known as *appropriation*. *Appropriation* invasion is all about the violation of the rights of individuals to control whether and how their names and likenesses are used for advertising and other publicity or commercial-related endeavors. If a person's photo, for example, is used in a promotional piece for some product, and the photo was run without the person's consent, he or she could sue on the basis of an *appropriation* invasion of privacy.

In a tiny nutshell, then, we have seen the various standards of invasion of privacy that are used to determine liability. If you feel you are a very clear victim of invasion of privacy and that said invasion has been injurious to either you or your family in some way, it may pay to find a lawyer who will be willing to talk to you for free. Although attorneys are generally very expensive, they are oftentimes willing to forgo their upfront fee, or retainer, if you present them with a very appealing opportunity. If, however, you are simply seeking a measure of personal protection and don't want to bother with the standard legal process, you can still get some mileage out of assuming an adversarial stance against the offending party. The best way to do this is to construct a professional letter outlining both your grievances as well as your demands, and send it to the individual, newspaper, TV station, or other entity which is the guilty party. Be specific when talking about which type of invasion of privacy standard you are citing. Show your knowledge! If you demonstrate that you know what you're talking about, it's very likely that you will have your demands met. (Be reasonable, though; don't ask for a million dollars. If you believe your case warrants that kind of demand, you should be speaking with a lawyer.) Finally, when you send your letter, always send it to the highest-ranking person in the corporation or business that you can, and make sure you mail it "return receipt requested." Show 'em right from the get-go that you mean business.

 Understand your rights and responsibilities as a pet owner.

This aspect of law does not really provide a mechanism for engaging in a defense without the services of an attorney. Nevertheless, it is important, and because so many people in this country are pet owners, I feel that it is of some value to you to know how the courts view your rights and responsibilities with respect to the ownership of animals you maintain on your premises.

If you are the owner of a common household pet—a cat, dog, goldfish, horse, and so on—courts have generally maintained that unless you have prior knowledge that said animal is dangerous, you are not responsible if the pet injures someone. This may come as a surprise to some of you who probably have believed that if the animal attacks or otherwise injures anyone, even if it's the first known attack, the owner is in big trouble. Not true. However, there is a generally accepted money saver of liability law with respect to pet ownership known as the "one-bite rule," which basically states that if you have prior knowledge of even one attack committed by the pet and the pet attacks again, you can be held liable for that second incident.

If you own an exotic pet of some kind, or an animal that is generally regarded as wild, you do not enjoy the grace period afforded by the "one-bite rule." Courts hold that owners of animals other than those regarded as being of the common household variety must adhere to a higher standard of public safety concern. If you own a poisonous snake or an alligator, for example, any incident involving the animal will absolutely translate into immediate liability for the pet owner.

One of the more common issues that arises in connection with this area of the law has to do with the pet owner's liability in the event the animal attacks a trespasser. Many people are under the impression that a trespasser assumes full responsibility for the risk of being attacked because he is on the property without permission. That is not true. Common sense dictates that there are varying degrees of trespasser, from the delivery boy to the burglar (or worse), and the courts agree. Therefore, the simple act of a person being on the property of another does not allow for the victimization of the trespasser. However, as you would expect, courts do account for circumstances in these matters. If your dog bites a trespasser who is on your property committing a crime, it is unlikely that the court will hold you responsible. Be advised, though, that even in such a case, the standard does not become one of "anything goes." Your animal may not injure the burglar or other criminal with a greater degree of trauma than is necessary to subdue or fend him off.

One step you *can* take to help limit your liability in these matters is to post clearly visible warning signs (such as "Beware of Dog"). Some of these signs even have a picture of a vicious-looking dog to warn people who can't read or who speak a different language. (These are the best ones to get.)

Demand satisfaction
from slow-mailing merchants.

If you're someone who likes the convenience of purchasing merchandise through mail order, you've likely made such purchases many times. If that's the case, then on probably more than one occasion you've found yourself having to wait an inordinately long period of time to receive your item(s). There may even have been a time or two when you never received the merchandise at all. A large number of people believe there's little they can do in such circumstances, that if they choose to purchase something long-distance they are assuming such risks.

Nonsense. There are important rights that all Americans enjoy with respect to the purchase of goods and services via mail order, and they pertain, in part, to the specific problem of delays in delivery of the merchandise. As with all of these other areas, the key to successfully fighting back lies with your knowledge of these rights and how you exercise them. Whatever you do, don't settle for less than absolute satisfaction. These companies certainly don't waste any time depositing your check; why should you allow them to drag their heels in delivering your purchases?

The Federal Trade Commission (FTC) threw down the gauntlet regarding mail-order merchandise in 1976. Basically, the FTC stated that it is deceptive and unlawful for a merchant/seller who is using the mails for his solicitation to make that solicitation if he cannot expect to ship the ordered merchandise within a reasonable period of time. If you've ever ordered anything by mail, you've likely noticed that the estimated length of delivery time is indicated somewhere in or on the advertisement. If it's not, the FTC's position is that the seller must ship the merchandise no later than 30 days after receipt of the order. Furthermore, if the seller determines that he cannot ship the merchandise in accordance with the guidelines outlined above, he must promptly and of his own accord offer the purchaser either a refund or the choice to agree to a longer shipping delay. One more thing, the FTC allows for you, in this circumstance, to change your mind at any time and opt for a refund even if you initially chose to wait.

In general, if someone willfully wrongs you in some way, it's often because he thinks he can get away with it. This notion is probably nowhere more applicable than it is to this subject. Mail order houses often assume (and, unfortunately, do so quite correctly) that the purchaser has no clue as to what his rights are under the law. In the case of mail order delay, however, you now do. The next phase of our discussion concerns precisely what steps should be taken to exercise those rights.

The first thing you should do is contact the seller by certified letter to demand a refund or shipment of the merchandise by a particular date. Furthermore, regardless of which option you select, you should also ask in your letter for an explanation as to why the FTC regulations have not been adhered to by them regarding this matter. You might even want to mention what those regulations are. This can be a very effective part of your letter because it demonstrates to the seller that you are aware of your rights and that you know where to go to file a complaint if you don't receive satisfaction.

The next step you should take, assuming the above action yields no results, is to make a formal complaint to the FTC. Again, send your letter by certified mail, making sure to give the complete details of your interaction with the seller in question from the get-go. Write or contact the FTC at:

Consumer Protection Bureau
Attention: Marketing Practices Division
Federal Trade Commission
6th and Pennsylvania Avenue, NW
Washington, DC 20580
(202) 326-2222

Finally, you may want to contact the Office of the Attorney General in your state and lodge a complaint as well. I advise you to initiate this option concurrently with your initiation of the complaint to the Federal Trade Commission. Your state's Office of the Attorney General can be very helpful in these matters, and they can greatly assist you in getting a refund *without* you having to hire an attorney.

In the event you choose to receive refunds in these situations, be advised that the seller must issue your refund by first-class mail within seven working days from the date you notified the seller of your choice. If the purchase was made by credit card, the seller has one billing cycle from the date he was notified that you wanted a refund to credit your account.

 Defend yourself against false or misleading advertising.

You have just read about how the Federal Trade Commission acts as a watchdog over the mail order business, and how you can use the FTC to demand satisfaction from mail-order sellers who don't deliver as they should. You should also know that the FTC has the authority to supervise advertising practices of sellers—whether they advertise through the mail or not. While the regulations issued by the FTC are very specific and at times complex (what government regulations aren't?), it can be said that the FTC deems unlawful any claim or description about a product or service that would mislead any reasonable consumer.

There are countless numbers of examples of false or misleading. Since we've all seen false claims and promises in ads, I don't want to take up a lot of space describing the wide variety of examples. However, there are a few important elements of this area of law that need to be mentioned, at least in a general sense.

It might surprise you to know that an advertiser cannot dodge liability for false and/or misleading advertising simply by placing a disclaimer somewhere in the body of the ad. Courts have clearly held that while disclaimers are certainly allowable in advertisements, if the disclaimer is not prominent within the advertisement and its wording and/or placement within the ad confuses the consumer or leaves him uncertain about the claims being made, then it's very likely that the advertising would be regarded as deceptive—and therefore unlawful. Many consumers feel they should always be cognizant of the fine print, and that if it's in there, it's their own responsibility to locate it. That's not completely true. If the fine print is too fine, or if what it says seems to contradict in some way the claims being made in the principal body of the advertisement, a deception may exist. If that's the case, the advertiser is liable.

Also, you might be interested to know that just because the vast majority of an advertisement is completely accurate, any inaccuracy, no matter how slight, can be used to deem the entire ad deceptive and hence unlawful.

One point you can take from all of this is that the days of "let the buyer beware" are quickly fading into history. While I personally believe that a buyer should accept responsibility for his purchase decisions, I believe that should be true only as long as the buyer has been given a complete and accurate picture of what he is purchasing before he lays down his money.

If you feel that you are the victim of false or misleading advertising, I suggest following the same course of action as outlined in the last section on mail order delivery delays. Again, the FTC and your state's Office of the Attorney General are excellent resources to use in obtaining satisfaction because they can help you receive a refund without you having to hire an attorney. First, though, contact the seller/advertiser yourself by certified letter, outlining your grievance and indicating your demands. Give them a chance to make the problem right first. Then, if you don't get the results you're seeking, call in the big guns.

*Demand satisfaction
if you are libeled.*

Not infrequently we have occasion to hear one person or another, angry about what another said about them, threaten to sue for libel. It seems that these folks rarely follow through on such threats, but that the threats are made in the first place seems to show that a good number of us are aware of the fact that we cannot make degrading or defaming statements about someone with impunity.

To open our discussion, we need to understand the difference between *libel* and *slander*. Libel refers to written statements, while slander refers to those statements made orally. I'm going to concentrate this discussion on libel in particular because slander, by its very nature, is tough to prove. Oral statements made about someone are typically not heard far and wide, so victims of slander have had a tough time proving in court that they are entitled to damages.

Libel is a different matter, however. A libelous statement that appears in a newspaper, for example, can easily be seen by thousands, even millions of people. Also, because the statement is made in print, its existence is easy to prove. Still, for a statement to be considered libelous in the eyes of the law, it must pass several tests. To begin with, the statement must be an accusation against one's character that impacts his reputation and holds him in ridicule or disgrace. This is the foundation of a libelous statement. However, that's not enough; the statement must pass four more tests. First, the statement has to be false; second, the statement has to be published (*published* in this case enjoys a very liberal definition; it refers to a statement in writing made to at least one other person. This could be as wide in scope as that which appears in a newspaper or magazine, or as narrow as that which appears in a simple letter from one individual to another); third, the person alleging libel has to be living (you cannot sue for libel on behalf of your deceased brother); and fourth, the person alleging libel has to have suffered injury by virtue of the statement. As you might imagine, it is this last stipulation that can make libel difficult to prove in court. Furthermore, you can be assured that most judges jealously guard the Bill of Rights in the United States' Constitution. Oftentimes suing for libel puts one at odds with the First Amendment, which has been interpreted through the years as providing expansive protection to a wide range of speech and communication.

Nonetheless, if you believe you have been libeled, you'll want to preserve or get back your good name. Although libel can be tough to prove in court, most book publishers and written media outlets do not want to have to deal with a libel suit if at all possible. It can cost a lot of money to defend against, and no business likes to face the unfortunate publicity that goes along with libel lawsuits. Accordingly, it's possible for you to realize satisfaction if you've been libeled simply by writing a letter to the offending publisher and/or person, detailing both the basis for your claim and your demands. As was the case in our prior discussion of invasion of privacy, do not use this method to make a demand for one million dollars. (If you feel your case is strong enough that you could potentially collect that much in a court, you need to retain a lawyer.) Remember, your letter should be clear and concise. To make it more effective you should list the above-named tests for determining libel and explain how your situation satisfies each. As always, send the letter via certified mail.

Before we close on this subject, you might be interested to know that there is one more requirement that must be met before *public figures* can sue for libel successfully. Public figures, who may be defined as those people whose names are well-known in the community and beyond, must be able to prove that the person or company making the statement either knew the statement to be false or didn't care whether it was false or not. This standard differs from the one applied to those people who are not public figures; for Mr. and Mrs. Average, simple negligence or an insufficient verification of facts or sources will do.

> *Know what constitutes a promise before you make—or break—one.*

The simple yet poignant act of promising to do something has probably been a part of all of our lives many times. Every day, all over the world, in the course of casual conversation, kids are making promises to their parents, parents are making promises to their children, and, of course, adults are promising all sorts of things to one another. So often we've heard the phrase "promises are made to be broken," and indeed, it seems that they so often are. But when are promises *not* made to be broken? Is it really possible in this day and age to use the courts to enforce a promise that has been made to you? The answer is yes, as long as the promise meets certain requirements.

In the eyes of the law, there must be *consideration* between two parties for a promise to be legally enforceable. Consideration, in the legal sense of the word, means that both parties have to give something up as a condition of the promise. For example, if you promise your friend that you'll give him half the money you earn washing cars, your friend cannot enforce that promise because there is no consideration; he is not giving you anything in return. The law regards promises to give what are basically gifts unenforceable. However, if you promise to split your earnings with him if he'll pay for the soap, then what you have is an enforceable promise. There is consideration on both sides; you agreed to part with half of your earnings, while he agreed to pay for the supplies.

You may have noticed that what makes a promise enforceable is that it must really be, for all intents and purposes, a contract. Use of the word *promise* in striking the deal is not considered nearly as relevant as whether both parties have agreed to concede something to one another.

Consideration can come in a variety of forms. Courts have held that there is consideration if someone refrains from pursuing a course of action because he has been promised the availability of another. If a prospective employer tells you that he will hire you in three weeks, and because of that statement you turn down other job offers, consideration exists. You gave up other verifiable job opportunities, one of which you surely would have taken, if you hadn't already been told you were hired by the aforementioned employer. If in three weeks the employer changes his mind and doesn't hire you, it is likely that the law would rule that the employer's promise to hire you is legally enforceable.

The bottom line, then, is that consideration in some form must exist between two parties for a promise to be enforceable. However, that may not be the end of it. Certain types of promises, depending upon the state in which they're made, may have to meet other requirements in order to be enforced. Usually, one of the other requirements is that the promise must be made in writing. You will want to contact the Office of the Attorney General in your state to see which of the following apply, but here is a list of the types of promises which, in some states, must be in writing in order to be enforceable.

Obligations of children: In general, obligations of persons under age 18 are not enforceable and may only become enforceable if the parties renew the terms of the promise as adults. However, in some states, this renewed agreement would have to be in writing in order to be enforceable.

Promises to pay the debts of another: In almost every state in the Union, a promise to pay the debt(s) of another is unenforceable unless it's in writing.

Real-estate transactions: In almost every state, agreements involving the buying and selling of real estate must be in writing to be considered enforceable.

Bankruptcy-related debts: In some states, a promise by a debtor to pay a debt that would have been discharged by bankruptcy is not enforceable unless it's in writing.

Long-term property leases: In most states, real-estate leases of lengths longer than one year's time must be in writing to be enforceable.

Promises relating to will provisions: Very often parties will strike bargains with one another whereby one person agrees to do something for someone or give something to that person, with the understanding that the second person will leave something of value to the first person in return. In some states, these kinds of agreements are unenforceable unless they're in writing.

Promises which by their terms will not be fulfilled within one year: If you make a promise that, by its terms, lasts more than one year's time, that promise is not enforceable in most states unless it's in writing. An example of this type of agreement might be when one person promises to pay the college tuition of another for four full years of college.

 Know your rights if you lose something.

There is a commonly held belief that if you lose something, by consequence you give up ownership of the item and, thus, no longer have any right to it. That is not true. On this subject, the law distinguishes between property that has been lost and property that has been abandoned. Let's examine the difference more closely.

The law maintains that when property is abandoned, it does not have an owner. This is because the action that left the property dispossessed was intentional on the part of the owner. Although there are lots of examples of abandonment, a common example is that of someone who vacates a premise, like an apartment, and leaves items behind. By willfully relinquishing possession of the items, the owner has abandoned the property and forsaken his claim to it. When property is lost, however, the law maintains that the person who was the owner at the time of the loss is *still* the owner and thus maintains his claim to the property.

Another misconception which is widely held has to do with the idea of "finders, keepers." If you come upon lost property, the law does not permit you to assert a claim to the property before you have made a reasonable effort to find the owner. If you come upon a wallet lying on the ground, the wallet and its contents are not yours to do with as you please in the eyes of the law. The law demands that you make a reasonable effort to find the wallet's owner, which could be done easily by opening the wallet and looking for some identification. If the lost property you find is something on behalf of which a search for an owner would not be a realistic undertaking, like a valuable necklace, then you can assert your claim to the item, except in that case the rightful owner may come forward and reclaim the property within the appropriate timeframe established by the relevant statute of limitations.

 If divorce is inevitable, strive for a cheap alternative.

I'm always a little skittish about discussing divorce because I'm concerned that some readers may interpret my willingness to discuss it as a gesture that I condone the practice. While I do not believe in divorce, and think that no-fault divorce laws in this country should be made more stringent in order to give more marriages a chance, I do recognize that divorce is an issue commonly faced by Christian as well as non-Christian couples. On that basis, I don't feel it's inappropriate to provide some advice that might help divorcing couples save a bundle of money in their ordeal.

Let me say right off the bat that if your impending divorce is at all contested, meaning that you and your spouse are not in total agreement on the terms of the split and thus will be litigating, you probably don't have much of an alternative but to hire an attorney. However, because divorce litigation can be expensive and emotionally trying, it pays to see if both of you are willing to sit down and try to hammer out mutually acceptable agreements as to the terms of the divorce. In many states there are laws for uncontested divorce that allow spouses who are in agreement to get it done quickly and cheaply. Although you may feel there's just no way you'll sit down with your spouse and discuss these matters, remember that divorce lawyers' fees can run into the thousands very quickly.

If you find that your divorce will indeed take place, investigate various options to make your experience as financially painless as possible. You will find, for example, that simple, uncontested divorces can be handled primarily by paralegals. This will save you a bundle in attorney fees. Also, if you have no money, you may qualify to be represented by attorneys who handle divorces on a pro-bono basis. To find out more about that, contact your state's bar association. Finally, although you should always be careful when considering this type of option, it is possible to avail yourself of do-it-yourself divorce materials. Nolo Press is a publishing house that specializes in the creation of forms and other materials that help people enact legal transactions on their own without the services of an attorney. You may contact Nolo Press at (800) 992-6656.

 Know your rights
before you're evicted.

Although I've had the very good fortune never to experience this, I think homelessness is one of the most frightening, most demeaning trials anyone may ever face. It's bad enough when you're on your own as an adult, but the prospect of homelessness must be downright terrifying when little children are involved. If you are a renter who is facing eviction, you probably are frantically searching for a way you can stave off the impending doom. Renters facing eviction do have some recourse, but, as with all rights, you have to know what they are and the best way to assert them.

The law maintains that there are basically three kinds of evictions. The first is perhaps the most common, and it is the type where you are *evicted for the nonpayment of your rent.* There is another type of eviction that is referred to as *for cause eviction.* It pertains to the violation of lease terms by the tenant. Keeping a dog at a residence where no pets are allowed or causing public disturbances within the community are two good examples of the kinds of behavior which typically justify this type of action. Finally, a *holdover eviction* can take place when a renter has overstayed his welcome; in other words, when he does not vacate the premises once his lease has expired. Although specific reasons for eviction may abound, the likelihood is that they fall into one of the three main categories of eviction outlined above.

Evictions in this day and age must take place in the form of an official legal process. Gone are the days when a landlord could simply remove you from the property on his own (called a *self-help eviction*), throwing you and your property out on to the street. In order to legally evict a tenant, the landlord must provide a *notice of eviction.* This notice must contain two principal pieces of information: The official notification that legal proceedings have been initiated and the reason(s) for the eviction. However, it should be mentioned that in some states no notice is required in cases of holdover eviction. The notice of eviction will contain a date when the renter is to appear in court. How you handle this court appearance which can make or break your effort to stay where you are.

First of all, show up! A lot of renters who are facing eviction simply do not appear at the courthouse at the appointed date and time, and you can be certain that the judge will order the eviction. This is important because often it's possible for tenants who show up in court and acquit themselves well to buy more time at the hands of the judge. Best of all, this can be done effectively without you having to hire a lawyer—but you should expect to do some homework beforehand. If you are being evicted because you are accused of being a noisy neighbor, for example, you might want to locate a few of your neighbors who would be willing to testify that you are *not* noisy (at least as far as they know) and are a perfectly reasonable and welcome member of that community. Nonpayment of rent is a little tough to get around, but if you can demonstrate mitigating financial circumstances and that your situation will change very soon, you may find that you'll get to spend a little more time in your place of residence. However, judges understand the plights of landlords and the fact that if you don't pay your rent, they may not be able to pay theirs, so don't expect much "kid glove" treatment here.

One way you can help stave off eviction for nonpayment of rent is to show that the landlord has done a poor job maintaining the property. Every landlord has a responsibility to provide a residence that meets or exceeds minimum levels of habitability. Examples of inhabitability abound, but basically, if you're not getting what you paid for, you have a good defense. You will want to take photographs of the problem areas and even have inspection reports in hand from appropriate regulatory authorities whom you have called to examine the property. Don't underestimate the effectiveness of this. If your landlord has not been maintaining the property to an acceptable standard, and you can demonstrate some proof of this, it is quite possible that the eviction proceedings will be terminated and you'll get another chance.

Protect your dignity with a living will.

While few of us could imagine anything worse than death, the fact is there are times when death would probably be welcomed by many. If you were involved in a serious automobile accident, for example, and could only be sustained by extreme and artificial measures that would keep you alive in only the most clinical sense, you might opt to forgo those procedures if you had the ability to do so. For many people, the idea of being kept alive by life-support systems when there's no reasonable chance for the resumption of a life anywhere near normal is quite distasteful. A lot of people object to such measures on the basis that it robs them of their dignity, reducing them to being little more than an extension of the very machine to which they're attached. A lot of Christians, especially, find this kind of state objectionable because they believe it interferes with the cycle of life as it has been developed by and of God.

Because there's no way for you to communicate your wishes in this regard once you have fallen into a vegetative or similar incapacitating state, you must do so beforehand. To do this legally, you must have a living will in place. A living will is a relatively simple document that basically authorizes a specific person to make medical decisions on your behalf when you are not able to do so. This can include, if you dictate it in the will, the power to terminate any artificial life-sustaining measures that may be put in place, or to refuse on your behalf extraordinary measures designed to keep you alive if it is felt by the medical staff and other relevant experts that there is no reasonable chance for recovery.

From a legal standpoint, you'll find that most states now recognize what is commonly referred to as the "right to die." However, not all states are in agreement as to how that right should be exercised. In a majority of states, you'll find that a basic living will, in fact one which might be considered a "do-it-yourself" living will, shall suffice to meet their standards. However, in the remaining states, things are not quite so simple. Some states require that a specific form be used, while in others the very issue of the living will has not been settled with any real clarity. If you're not certain about your own state's position on the living will, there are a number of resources you can contact which should be able to help you, including the state bar association or perhaps a local hospital. Assuming living wills are enforceable in your state, it's likely that bookstores or the local library will have the form you need to do this correctly. I recommend that you contact the National Council for the Right to Die at 200 Varick St., 10th Fl., New York, NY 10014 (212) 366-5540 and ask for their assistance. They will have the information, including standardized forms, you require to proceed in this matter.

 Understand the legal definition of negligence.

Negligence. We hear that word all of the time, and its use seems to have grown exponentially in the last 10 to 20 years as more and more people look to the civil courts as a means to wealth. If someone suffers adverse consequences of any kind for any reason, the first thing we try to determine is who was at fault. That makes sense. What doesn't make sense, though, is some of the ways the law has seen fit to ascribe. It seems as though the interpretation of negligence by the law can sometimes run contrary to what a reasonable person might presume it to be.

In order to sue someone for negligence, the negligent party must pass four tests at the outset. First, it has to be felt that the negligent person had a duty to other people; second, it has to be felt that the person failed in this duty; third, the failure to live up to the duty caused an injury to another person; and fourth, the injury caused a financial loss to the injured party.

This test, or legal definition, seems simple enough. However, the practical application of negligence has not proven to be so straightforward. There has evolved two types, or standards, of legal negligence over the years, and some states use one, while some use the other. The first type we'll discuss is *contributory negligence*, while the other type is *comparative negligence*.

The doctrine of *contributory negligence* basically states that if it can be shown that a plaintiff was even slightly at fault for his own injuries, then he can collect nothing. For example, if a pedestrian steps on a shovel that was left on a sidewalk by a municipal worker and was injured, he may not be able to recover any damages in states that maintain the doctrine of contributory negligence. The reason? Well, even though the worker and the ramifications of his actions would surely pass each part of the four-step test for negligence outlined above, it might well be shown that the plaintiff failed in his duty to himself by not doing a better job of watching where he was going. Surely, some might argue, if he had been watching out, there's no way he would have allowed himself to step on a shovel that was obviously lying in his path. As a result, it's clear that the plaintiff bears some measure of the responsibility for his own injuries. In states that support the standard of contributory negligence, the plaintiff in this example would not likely be able to recover any damages.

While the standard of contributory negligence, if alive and well in all 50 states, would surely keep the cost of insurance way down, it has come to be replaced through the years in a majority of states by the doctrine of *comparative negligence*. By this standard, plaintiffs can successfully sue for damages even if it's shown that they bear some measure of the responsibility for their injuries. However, the standard of comparative negligence has been applied differently by different states through the years. For example, in some states, juries are asked to ascribe fault between plaintiffs and defendants in percentages, and this can be difficult. For example, in our previous example of the pedestrian and the shovel, comparative negligence would require that some percentage of fault lies with the defendant, while some percentage might lie with the plaintiff. The question is, how much lies with whom? Comparative negligence seems like a fairer doctrine than contributory negligence, but it does open the Pandora's box of interpretation and subjectivity to a much greater degree. However, it should be noted that except in a very few states, plaintiffs cannot recover on the basis of comparative negligence if it can be shown that they were at least 50 percent at fault for their injuries. Let's look at our shovel–pedestrian example again. Let's assume that the shovel was *not* left on the sidewalk, but was positioned right by the worker and right next to the hole he was digging. Let's also say that the hole was a good 40 feet from the sidewalk. Let's assume as well that the pedestrian, for whatever reason, abandoned walking on the sidewalk and walked near the hole, then he stepped on the shovel. A good case could be made in this scenario that the pedestrian was at least 50 percent responsible for his injuries. If that were held to be true, he could not collect anything in a state that supports the doctrine of comparative negligence.

The doctrine of comparative negligence, overall, seems to be a fair way to go. There's still room for improvement, however. In a few states, it's actually possible for a plaintiff to recover damages even if it's shown that he was almost entirely responsible for his injuries; in other words, the "equal to or greater than 50 percent" rule does not apply.

If you are not certain which doctrine of negligence the civil courts in your state adhere to, you would do well to find out. A call to the state bar association or the Office of the Attorney General should clear that up for you in a jiffy.

*Know your responsibilities
to guests in your home.*

From time to time, the subject of a homeowner's legal responsibilities to his guests will arise in the courts for one reason or another. As with many legal concepts, this area is replete with misconceptions held by laypeople about what a homeowner's responsibilities are. The first thing to know is that, in the eyes of the law, there are two types of visitors to your premises: licensees and invitees. Let's look at the differences between the two and detail the homeowner's responsibilities to each.

A licensee is basically a social guest, one who is presumed to be on your property at your invitation or with your permission. Many people assume that guests of any kind enjoy a higher degree of protection from hazards than do family members, but the courts have not held that to be true. As a result, very few social guests, or licensees, have sued their hosts and enjoyed any degree of success in the process. There is, however, an exception: children. Even if children are social guests and thus considered technically to be licensees, the courts have held that the little tykes *do* enjoy a higher degree of protection than their adult counterparts, for reasons which should be obvious.

Invitees are visitors to your property who are there for business purposes. If you run a business out of your home, like many people do these days, your clients and patrons enjoy a higher level of protection than do licensees in the eyes of the law. The reasoning used to support this notion is that the host, in his capacity as a business owner or operator, is receiving financial benefits from his visitors. As a result, the law requires the host of invitees to exercise a higher degree of care and diligence with respect to their well being and safety.

In general, you will want to ensure that your property is as hazard-free as possible. Courts have found invitee hosts to be held liable for the injuries of their guests even when said guests were injured as a result of hazards encountered when they were in a part of the premises that had nothing to do with the function of the business. However, you should know that there is a slowly developing trend among the courts in a number of states to hold hosts of licensees to the same standard of liability as hosts of invitees. In other words, the courts are beginning to support the misconception we spoke about in the beginning of this piece. If you do operate a business out of your home (and even if you don't), you may want to consider contacting local authorities such as the fire inspector or building inspector to get some guidance regarding what types of safeguards you should have in place for the benefit of your guests. This way, if trouble arises, you can demonstrate that you exercised due diligence in providing for the safety and welfare of your guests.

 Protect your rights by learning about the statutes of limitations.

Our country gives us the opportunity to seek redress through the civil courts for wrongs we feel have been done to us, but the states in which we live don't normally give us forever to use that mechanism. Statutes of limitations, which are the laws that dictate how long we have to pursue legal action, can vary widely depending upon both the area of the law in question (negligence, medical malpractice, assault, written contracts, and so on) and the state's requirements. You can contact your state's Office of the Attorney General to discover the different statutes of limitations that pertain to the area of the law you're concerned about. They'll be happy to give you guidance. What I want to do here is make you aware of the more common reasons regarding when and why statutes of limitations can be circumvented to the benefit of prospective plaintiffs. Again, this outline is intended to be a general review of this subject; specific questions regarding your own situation should be directed to the aforementioned Office of the Attorney General.

There are certain circumstances that allow for the statutes of limitations to be "tolled" from time to time. When the statute of limitations is "tolled," it means that the countdown clock, which keeps track of the time limit for initiating a suit, begins ticking only after a mandated period of delay. Young people are often recipients of this benefit, as statutes of limitations usually don't kick in until a person reaches adulthood. For example, if a person under the age of 18 suffers any injury for which he could sue, and the normal statute of limitations for the area of the law that applies in this case is five years to initiate the suit, the statute is "tolled" until he reaches the age of majority (18). So, if he suffers his injury at age 14, he doesn't have until just age 19 to sue; in his situation, the statute is tolled until he reaches 18, which means he has until age 23 to sue.

There are, in fact, several reasons why statutes of limitations may be legally tolled. If a person suffers from mental illness, the clock doesn't begin ticking until that point when he or she is adjudged sane. Also, if a prospective plaintiff has been in prison, the applicable statutes are tolled until his release date. If a prospective plaintiff has been absent from the state for a period of time, said absence may cause the applicable statute to be tolled. Although just about every commonwealth and state make tolling allowances based on considerations for mental illness, imprisonment, youth, absence, and legal incompetence, it should be noted that at last check Puerto Rico made no such allowances. Also, in some states, statutes of limitations that are subject to tolling also may decrease the allotted time for action. For instance, a three-year time limitation for initiating a suit may be shortened to two years if it has been tolled.

One more thing. Be advised that in some cases, when you enter into a contract with another party, a condition of that contract may be that you waive the statute of limitations for the benefit of the party requesting the waiver. This means that the other party may sue you years down the road, even if the normal statute of limitations has expired. In many states, it is legal for someone to waive their rights as they pertain to statutes of limitations regarding contracts. If you have a question, don't hesitate to contact your state's Office of the Attorney General *before* you sign on the dotted line.

 Yes, you can enforce an implied warranty.

Most of the warranties with which we're familiar as consumers are written. We see them most frequently whenever we buy such things as household appliances and consumer electronics, but they exist also with respect to cars, homes, and a variety of other big-ticket goods. While consumers and merchants have been known to haggle over the enforcement of a warranty when a defect arises in a purchased product, at least the written nature of the warranty gives both sides an obvious point of reference. But what rights do you have when the item you've purchased does *not* come with a written warranty? As a consumer, are you afforded any protection at all?

The simple answer is yes.

A warranty that is not written is known in legal terms as an *implied warranty.* Some of you may be thinking, "How do I know if I'm receiving one? Does the merchant have to announce it?" Not at all. Every time you buy something from a merchant who makes his living, at least in part, by selling that particular product, you receive an implied warranty. The Uniform Commercial Code (UCC) holds that there are two basic types of implied warranties: an implied warranty of merchantability and an implied warranty of fitness of purpose. An implied warranty of merchantability is the most basic. The UCC basically states that if you buy something from a merchant, an implied warranty that the purchased good(s) shall be "merchantable" now exists. (In general, the sale of something from one person to another is regarded as a contractual arrangement, since both sides have exhibited consideration: the merchant gives up the merchandise in exchange for the consumer giving up his or her money.) For something to be merchantable, it must be of "fair, average quality" or better.

Understanding the implied warranty of merchantability is important because it is the type of implied warranty we encounter most regularly. Many people are led to believe that if they buy a piece of merchandise for which a service contract is offered, but choose not to buy the service contract, then they have no recourse if the merchandise proves defective at some point. Under the implied warranty of merchantability, if you purchase a bracelet that soon breaks, you may return to the merchant and get a full refund. That a service contract on the bracelet was offered and refused at the time of sale in no way excuses the seller from his or her responsibility to live up to the terms of the implied warranty.

The other type of implied warranty that comes into play most regularly is the implied warranty of fitness of purpose. This usually deals with merchants who sell specialized products. The UCC basically says that if a seller of something comes to know at the time of sale that the consumer wants the merchandise to serve a particular purpose, and he knows that the buyer is relying on his expertise in the particular area of relevance to provide him with the right good for his purpose, then an implied warranty exists that dictates that the good(s) sold will be suitable for said purpose. For example, if you go into a consumer electronics store and ask the salesperson for the right kind of amplifier for the system you own currently, and he recommends one which later turns out to be incompatible, the implied warranty of fitness for a particular purpose was breached.

If you attempt to return merchandise because one of the above-referenced implied warranties was breached, you normally should not have a problem if the merchant is fair-minded and reasonable. If, however, he refuses to retake possession of the merchandise and return your money, know that you can handle the situation without going to an attorney. First, state to the store manager (leave the salesperson behind at this point) what the problem is, what your legal rights are under the UCC (you may want to mention the one that specifically applies in your case), and that you want satisfaction. If you don't get it at this level, don't conclude that you must hire an attorney to get your money back. Instead, persist in your efforts, taking your grievance to higher levels within the operation. Track down (which won't be difficult) the district manager, the regional manager, and any and all corporate officers you can. Send a letter (certified, of course) outlining your grievance, knowledge of your rights, and your demands (which should be no more than a return of your money). You may also state in the letter that you were very dismayed at the reaction to your grievance on the part of the manager with whom you spoke initially, and that if you don't receive satisfaction, you will lodge a formal complaint with your state's Office of the Attorney General as well as the Federal Trade Commission. Remember, many merchants are used to getting away with irresponsible business practices because the vast majority of Americans have no clue as to what their rights are nor how to see them enforced. When you demonstrate your knowledge of your rights you should get satisfaction immediately.

 Become familiar with zoning regulations.

The days of being able to do what you wish with your property are long gone. As society continues to progress rapidly and more and more Americans take up residence all over the United States, government at all levels has taken it upon itself to regulate the use of real estate by its citizenry. *Zoning* is the area of law having to do with the appropriate use of land by the people for residential, commercial, and industrial purposes. Zoning regulations can be divided up into three areas of concern: land use with respect to the intentions of the occupants/owners, the degree to which a particular area can be developed, and the specific dimensions and physical characteristics of the land, structures, parking facilities, and so on. For the purposes of this book, I'm going to limit the discussion to residential zoning concerns.

Zoning regulations and requirements for residents are usually developed and enforced at local government levels. In general, each municipality or county that governs zoning at some level will have a map that shows which areas are designated for what purposes, and the requirements of each. You can, however, ask the relevant zoning authorities in your community (often known as the zoning board or the planning board) for a "variance" if your intentions for a specific piece of property do not match the purposes and restrictions for that property zone. A variance is an "exception to the rule" made on your behalf.

There are a lot of reasons why you might request a variance. Perhaps you want to start a home-based business, but zoning regulations prevent you from setting up the kind of business you would like to have on your property. Maybe you want to build a guest house on your property, but the zoning regulations don't allow for an additional structure to be built there. All you have to do is request the variance. The process for seeking it does not require the assistance of an attorney. You can do it yourself; you just need to know the procedure.

The first step to obtaining a variance is to file an application with the appropriate authority, usually a committee in your community designated to handle zoning matters. The application is quite simple. Contact the planning or zoning board at issue and ask how they want the application to be made. Usually, they will be able to provide you with a preprinted application form. The application asks you basic information about yourself and your property and to indicate the reason you are seeking the variance, or adjustment as it is sometimes called.

When you file the application, it is reviewed by staff members whose job it is to advise the "top guns" in the authority on such matters. During this review process, it's quite possible that you may be asked to provide additional information pertaining to your request. Once the review is complete, the staff advisory committee makes a recommendation to the rest of the board as to whether they should accept or reject your request. The actual decision, however, is usually made in a public forum, at a meeting of the zoning/planning board. Your application is officially considered at a public hearing, the date and time of which you will be notified. If you can, it's a good idea to have some neighbors attend the hearing and testify in your behalf. For example, if you want to add a guest house or other structure to your property, it would help your cause if the board could hear your neighbors express their belief that the structure would not, in their opinion, detract from the appearance of the neighborhood.

If your request is denied, you have the right to file an appeal. The appeal process takes place at the same level as the original request. To file an appeal, you need to use a form similar to the one used to make the initial request. If your appeal is denied, it's possible to take the matter further, but at this point you will likely be faced with hiring an attorney. Therefore, you should do everything you can to win at the local level. To do this, do as much preparation as possible, taking absolutely nothing for granted. As long as your request falls within the boundaries of reason and you have gone to the trouble of clearly showing why you should be granted the variance, it's unlikely that you'll have much of a problem.

 Protect your business or product name with a trademark.

If you're in business and your business goes by a distinctive name or generates a specific product or provides a service that carries a distinctive name, it is in your best interest to make sure that no one usurps that name for his or her own purposes. This goal of proprietary protection is the motivating idea behind trademarks and servicemarks. As you work hard and your business grows, its name (or the name of the product or service generated) becomes the single most important identifier of it. Should someone else decide to go into the same business and take the name and, consequently, the reputation you've worked so hard to build, it could have devastating consequences for your future success.

The Lanham Act authorizes the United States Patent and Trademark Office to exercise jurisdiction over the registration of trademarks and service marks used in interstate commerce. For the record, it should be mentioned that trademarks pertain to goods, while service marks pertain to (surprise!) services (for the purposes of simplicity in our discussion, we'll talk only about trademarks, although everything said here about trademarks applies to service marks). You may trademark, and thereby protect as your own, words, symbols, devices, or any combination thereof when they are used to identify and distinguish specific goods and are distinctive of said goods. You may not, for example, trademark the word *water* by itself. You may, however, trademark the name "Joe's Sparkling Water" because that name is distinctive.

Although there are attorneys out there who specialize in this kind of law (and even those who don't who would nonetheless be happy to trademark something for you), you can trademark something on your own without much difficulty. The first step you need to take is to contact the Patent and Trademark Office (PTO) at (703)308-4357 and request an application. The application is not too tedious and comes in a packet that includes explicit instructions on how to complete it. Furthermore, you may call the trademark office if you have any questions while filling out the application. Once completed, you'll want to return it, along with any supporting documents and materials that are requested and a check for $245* to the Patent and Trademark Office. The PTO will determine if the applied-for mark is sufficiently distinctive and appropriate enough to warrant protection and will let you know of that decision approximately three months following the date of application. After that, there comes a period of

---

* You might want to call the PTO at (703) 308-4357 for an update on fees.

time whereby anyone with a similar mark or who feels he has a justifiable reason for opposing the mark may do so. Once that period of time goes by without complication, the mark is registered and the owner of the mark enjoys the protection for 20 years. The mark can be renewed indefinitely for 10-year terms at the conclusion of the first 20-year protection period. If anyone violates your registered rights under the trademark laws, you may obtain an injunction that prevents them from using the mark and sue for triple damages.

 Fight traffic citations without a lawyer.

Even if you're a good, careful driver, the chances are fairly decent that you may be the recipient of a traffic citation sooner or later. If you agree with the police officer's determination that you deserve a ticket, fine. Pay the cost of the ticket, attend a state-sponsored driver improvement course, or choose any of the other options that are available to drivers who have been ticketed for a traffic violation and agree they are guilty of the stated infraction. What should you do, however, if you *don't* agree with the actions of the officer and believe you should not have received the ticket? Many people pay the fine anyway, believing they could never be successful challenging the ticket or that they would have to hire a lawyer to do so. The truth is, you may have great success fighting the ticket, and you can do so without hiring an attorney. All you need to do is make a date . . . with traffic court!

Because there are countless numbers of traffic citations handed out every day of every week of every year, the states created a separate court system for dealing with these matters. Given the nature of the offenses and punishments at stake in traffic court, it is no big deal for a layperson to represent himself in this arena. (If you have been arrested for an alcohol-related driving offense or another serious charge, you *should* seek the services of an attorney). The key to success, as in any other instance where you are acting as your own legal representative, is to be prepared.

If it is your intention to fight the ticket, you should begin contacting witnesses who are available to back up your story. If you have some witnesses who would be of assistance but can't appear with you at the appointed date and time, you need to show up anyway so you can ask the judge for a continuance (a postponement).

If you do not seek a postponement, the judge will ask how you plead. If you wish to plead "not guilty," the case will proceed. You should remember that you and your witnesses will face a state prosecutor in the course of your defense, so you need to make sure you and your companions are well prepared and that everyone has reviewed his or her testimony. After the testimony, the judge (or jury if you've elected to go that route) gives his verdict, which you need to abide by.

It can also be worthwhile to show up in traffic court even if you are going to plead guilty. Although you can usually prepay your ticket through the mail, if you appear in court you can apprise the judge of any mitigating circumstances that led to the infraction. If you were arrested for speeding, for example, but were speeding because you found out your son had been taken to the hospital, make sure the judge knows that (be prepared to produce evidence of that claim). If you were arrested for reckless driving, but in fact had to swerve to avoid hitting a child, you should certainly be prepared to state that and back it up (that's why witnesses are so important, even if you are technically guilty of the infraction). The fact is, outside factors do influence the decision-making of traffic court judges.

One thing I want to put to rest is the notion that all you have to do is elect to appear in traffic court to beat the ticket because the arresting officer will probably not appear and the case will be dismissed. That *can* happen, but it happens a lot less than you might have been led to believe. First of all, the officer doesn't usually have the flexibility to not show up in court. He has a responsibility to the state to appear, and you can bet he will. If you do choose to fight a ticket in traffic court, do so with the intention of making a legitimate case in your defense.

Fight your own battles in small claims court.

If you are involved in a dispute for an amount of money that is relatively low, say no more than a few thousand dollars, you probably have a way in your state to seek redress without having to hire an attorney. Most states have small claims courts, which allow laypeople to sue and represent themselves in a court of law. You'll find that differences may exist from state to state with respect to the dollar amount limits over which people may sue in small claims court, and there may be some procedural differences, but in general, small claims courts are the same everywhere you go.

To initiate the process, you must file a statement of claim in which you indicate the nature of the dispute and the dollar amount for which you're suing. Once that's done, the defendant will be served with legal process, perhaps with a subpoena, which means he or she will be officially notified of the complaint. Once the statement of claim has been filed and the defendant has been served, the clerk of the court will set a date for the trial and notify both parties.

Small claims court is similar to other civil courts in some ways, and dissimilar in others. For example, the proceedings, while they do retain a measure of the formality you'll find in any courtroom, are a bit less regimented. In many places, a judge in a small room with only the relevant parties present hears the case. In such instances, it's not uncommon to find all parties sitting around a table, almost like a group of people engaging in an after-dinner discussion. The judge will give both sides their respective turns to make their cases, but you'll find that he'll give everyone a chance to say as much as possible. He will even give the people delivering testimony a lot of leeway in making informal statements and even engaging in conjecture to some extent, something which is generally not permitted in other civil courts. Once the judge is satisfied that he has heard enough to make a decision, he'll make it, often right then and there.

If you are considering initiating a suit in small claims court, there are some things you should remember. First of all, make sure that you have as much documentation as possible. Although a judge will be happy to hear a case that is based on an unwritten contract or agreement, for example, you should not be surprised in the least if he finds for the defendant. Also, when you show up at the court, be as well dressed as possible. Although the defendant should do the same, it looks worse if the person who initiated the action doesn't seem to care enough about the proceeding to ensure he looks his best. If you're a man, you should always wear a suit with a tie, and a woman should dress as formally. Also, when delivering testimony, remember to be as respectful as possible to the judge, always referring to him as "Your Honor." When giving your testimony, remain calm at all times. Do not let your emotions get in the way of the job you're trying to do; do not shout at anyone in the courtroom (especially the judge!), and refrain from using foul language. Perhaps the best advice you'll get on the subject of preparation is to visit a small claims court a few days before your own proceeding is scheduled to take place and watch what happens. It would be best if you could get a chance to watch the proceedings in the courtroom of the judge who will be hearing your case so you can get a feel for his personality and style—and use what you learn to your advantage.

10

Great Trips;
Great Prices

I have been in every major U.S. city and have become "traveled out" at this point in my life. Don't get me wrong, traveling can be great fun. But, hey, when you live ten minutes from the beach and live on a golf course, why go anywhere else? Seriously though, despite the fact that I'm traveling less and using videoconferences and other means of business communication and media appearances, I still travel quite a bit. So I have much to share with you regarding ways to save.

Whether you travel for business or pleasure, the cost of traveling can be what really makes the difference between enjoying a successful trip or experiencing one you'd like to forget as quickly as possible. I'm going to show you a number of ways you can save money in just about every key facet of travel. A lot of these strategies are well-known within the travel industry, but not really publicized outside of it. As is usually the case, it takes some digging from an interested party to find the inside scoop on low-cost vacations. Fortunately, I can also draw on so much of what I have learned through my many years as a radio host of a variety of consumer financial talk shows. During these interviews, I had the privilege of talking with some of the top names in the consumer travel game, and the lessons they taught have been difficult to forget.

How can you more fully enjoy your time away from home? By keeping your travel-related costs down as far as possible. Without further adieu, let's go hunting for travel bargains.

Air Travel

For so many of us, traveling means flying. Through the years, airline tickets have been notoriously expensive, but the advent of discount airlines changed that somewhat. Nevertheless, flying, regarded as a lot safer than driving, is still quite expensive. There are, however, a great number of ways you can reduce the cost of your tickets.

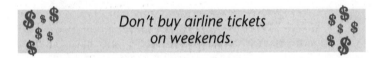

Don't buy airline tickets
on weekends.

If you can avoid doing so, resist buying airline tickets from Friday night through Sunday. Fewer airline tickets are sold on weekends than are sold during the week, and a lot of carriers take advantage of the slower sales to actually test fare increases and gauge the response. I know that may sound kind of strange to some of you, but it's very true. Once Monday rolls around, go back to buying your tickets as usual.

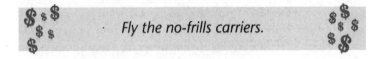

Fly the no-frills carriers.

No-frills flying is great for the person who just wants to get where he's going. There is no meal of any kind served, there are barely even snacks available, and the in-flight entertainment consists of watching the other passengers sweat and squirm in the cheap seats. However, you can save money—*a lot* of money—by taking the no-frills option. There are a lot of excellent no-frills airlines out there, even in the wake of the famous ValuJet crash that occurred a few years back. In fact, the pressure on no-frills airlines to maintain a high degree of safety has indirectly suggested that the safest place to fly right now is on a no-frills carrier!

If your destination is a smaller city, try the "hidden-city" ploy.

Airline fares can be very unusual in terms of how and why they cost what they do. It is not unusual to find a situation where the cost of a ticket from your location to a major city, which includes a layover at the city where you *really* want to go, is cheaper than what the cost of the ticket would be if you bought it specifically for that intermediate destination. If you find yourself in that circumstance, simply buy the ticket to the final destination, and deplane at the layover site. I can tell you up front that airlines are not terribly excited about passengers who do this, but there is nothing illegal or unethical about it.

If you must fly due to the death of a loved one, do not pay full-price.

If you're in the sad circumstance of having to fly to the funeral of a loved one, always do so with the benefit of what is known as a bereavement fare. As the name implies, a bereavement fare is a lower-cost fare charged by airlines to people who must travel to and from the funeral of a close relative. Just about all airlines will give you a break on the ticket in these situations (the discount will vary from 15 to 50 percent off), but you should contact the airline you're considering for details about their specific policies.

Avoid paying full-price for children's seats.

If you find yourself taking a family vacation that includes young children, ask if there are any discounts given on behalf of children's fares. American Airlines, for instance, will give a discount of roughly 50 percent off of full fare for children traveling domestically. International flights can see discounts of as much as 75 percent. It is possible, as well, to find airlines that will occasionally let kids fly for no cost at all, but those deals are only good if the child is accompanied by an adult paying the full fare for his ticket.

If the child happens to be a full-fledged baby, there is not going to be a charge if he is under the age of two and will be taking up residence during the flight on a parent's lap. More and more airlines, however, are requiring that babies have their own full-size seats into which child seats will fit for safety reasons. However, don't fret; fares for seats occupied by babies are usually less than 50 percent off the going rate.

Fly out of airports where the fares are cheaper.

If you have the luxury of living within the general proximity of at least two active airports, shop your fare around with each of them to see where your deal will be the cheapest. For example, a ticket from Orlando, Florida to Dallas, Texas was a lot more money at one time than a ticket from Clearwater, Florida to Dallas. Granted, I lived closer to Orlando, but because I was willing to drive the two hours necessary to fly out of the Clearwater location, I was able to save hundreds of dollars on the round-trip ticket. I realize this may be a hassle for some of you, but oftentimes saving money involves sacrificing a measure of convenience to secure a lower price.

Buy through a travel agent.

If you buy your ticket through a travel agent, you will have the benefit of buying from someone who can quickly and clearly tell you which airline has the best deal. Travel agents have special computer applications for these purposes, and one of the benefits is that they can shop around more quickly and accurately than you may be able to on your own.

 Take advantage of the Internet to secure your flight deal.

The Internet is revolutionizing so much of what we do and the way we do it. For example, it is now possible to buy airline tickets via your home computer by jumping on the Internet. If you subscribe to America Online, for example, you need only click on the travel channel that appears when you first log on, and you will be brought to sites where you can shop for the cheapest fare. Also available on the Internet is a new company called Priceline (www.priceline.com) where you can actually place bids for tickets that run to and from the locations you wish to travel. You can tell Priceline how much you want to pay for a ticket, and it will try to find a ticket for you at that price. If there is no match found, simply re-submit another bid that is a few dollars higher. Keep doing this until you get a match. Be forewarned, though, that the only consideration that service utilizes in its search is the price of the ticket, which means that to get the fare you want, you may have to fly at some very inconvenient times. Nevertheless, to be able to secure a ticket at a phenomenally low price may be well worth it.

If you're a senior citizen, look into discount coupon books.

If you're a senior citizen, you would do well to take advantage of the plethora of flying deals there are out there. Probably one of the best involves the purchasing of the coupon books airlines make available that drastically reduce the cost of otherwise full-price fares. The coupon books will vary in value and other specifics, so you will have to inquire of each airline to find out more of the information you'll need. Also, these coupon books can be purchased through travel agents. For most of these deals, you need to be at least age 62.

Save big on international travel by flying as an air courier.

If you yearn to fly to an international destination, but have little money to purchase the usually expensive ticket, or you simply wish to fly for an incredible deal, you may want to fly as an air courier. An air courier is someone who, essentially, agrees to give up his baggage space when he flies so that a courier company may check a piece of business cargo in its place. The reason companies do this is because time-sensitive materials, which need to get to destinations expeditiously, may languish for hours before clearing customs if sent as standard cargo. However, because passenger luggage is cleared much more quickly, courier companies like to use that avenue whenever possible.

Now, be advised that air courier travel is not the route you want to take if you are seeking a typical family vacation. First of all, there are few opportunities for couriers to fly with anyone else, so unless you're content traveling alone, this may not be for you. Also, because you're agreeing to give up luggage space, you will be limited in bringing personal items to what you can fit in carry-on luggage (and airlines have been cracking down on excesses in that area by passengers).

There are also other built-in restrictions that make air courier travel appropriate for only the heartiest individual traveler, but if you fit the bill, you may be able to fly to the exotic destinations you've always dreamed of for a dirt-cheap rate. Although it is possible to book air courier flights on your own, novices would probably want to do it through either of two well-known courier booking agencies: Discount Travel International at (212) 362-3636 and Now Voyager at (212) 431-1616. Make sure you have a passport in hand before you call because courier flights may leave on very short notice.

Hotel/Motel Rates

Although there are a lot of hotels and motels available to you and your wallet, there is also a wide disparity in quality as well. The key is to try to stay at a five-star location for a one-star price. Now, that won't really happen, but it is possible to pay a substantially lower rate on your hotel bill by incorporating some clever strategies.

 When reserving at a chain, call the specific location for a better deal.

Whenever you hear or see an advertisement for a hotel chain, you will usually be offered a toll-free number to call and receive more information or to make a reservation. However, if you know which hotel in the chain you specifically want to stay at, you will always be better served if you call the direct number for that location. The reason is that if you want to negotiate the standard rate, you're going to be out of luck by calling the central number. The reservationists who work there are not authorized to do anything but quote the standard rates and offer the standard discounts available through the chain (like auto club membership discounts, for example). Individual hotel managers, however, who will be under pressure from corporate offices to keep occupancy levels as high as possible, may be willing to let you have rooms for less money than is usually allowed. However, that is something you will have to take up with them directly, which you can't do through central reservations.

If you're a shareholder of the hotel chain, ask for a preferred rate.

If you invest in the stock market and own shares of the hotel chain where you want to stay, it never hurts to ask for a discount on that basis. This is a strategy that you'll want to employ *when you call first.* If the hotel says, "Okay," there will probably be some additional requirements for you to meet before getting the room for less money.

Ask for the corporate rate.

If you are a businessperson who happens to be traveling for pleasure, it doesn't hurt to ask for the corporate rate, anyway. How well this strategy works may depend on a couple of factors, such as the current demand for rooms. Of course, if you are traveling on business, you should certainly ask for the corporate rate.

Cut hotel costs by staying in business-oriented hotels on weekends.

If you've ever traveled on business, you know that there are hotels located near substantially sized office parks and business districts that cater specifically to the businessperson who travels there for work. But the occupancy levels of those same hotels plummet on weekends as the businesspeople return home. Accordingly, these locations often offer substantial discounts on weekend rates to try to boost occupancy. If you are traveling with your family or taking a vacation, it's a good idea to try to track down these hotels that are located at least in the general vicinity of where it is you want to be. A key to doing this is to look closely at various travel guides that specifically list hotels, as well as at the guides issued by the specific hotel chains in which you're interested. By spending some time checking, you should be able to identify those business hotel locations that are near where you want to be. Once you do, call the hotel(s) directly to see what discounts they offer to weekenders.

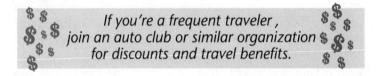

If you're a frequent traveler , join an auto club or similar organization for discounts and travel benefits.

A fair number of people out there know that by joining certain kinds of organizations, such as auto clubs, they can realize tremendous savings on a variety of travel and entertainment-related expenses, including hotel rates and rental car costs. Memberships in some of these organizations can be as little as $25 or $30 annually, and you can realize savings of ten times that (or more) in a single year when you use the special discounts available.

If you're considering joining an organization solely for the discount, make sure that you evaluate the entire list of benefits you will receive as a member *before* joining. In other words, don't assume that because you're joining a well-known organization, it will have benefits you will use.

Don't accept the first rate you are quoted when you walk into the lobby.

When you seek to rent a room for the evening, be mindful about being too compliant when you're quoted a rate. I would suggest that you thank the clerk when the standard rate is offered, and then tell him that you were wondering if there were any specials available, or if he could do any better than the price he quoted. This is a strategy that can be especially effective when you are walking into the hotel lobby late into the evening, and it happens that there are still a lot of vacancies. I can assure you that the clerk will almost always quote you the standard rate first to try to get you to rent the room at full price. Nevertheless, hotel managers know better than anyone that a room that brings in just 75 percent of the standard rate is still doing a lot better than one that remains unoccupied for the night. Managers will not likely let you get away with paying ridiculously low rates for these rooms, but you should be able to realize some significant savings.

Also, if you want to try to negotiate a better deal with the hotel manager or desk clerk, do not make the mistake of bringing your luggage into the lobby. Once you've done that, the staff knows that your inclination to want to take it back out to your car is already diminished significantly. They will feel (and will likely be right) that they have you by the tail. Keep your belongings in the car or outside the lobby so you aren't giving up any ground in the negotiation process.

Rent a room devoid of the special amenities.

Oftentimes when you peruse a hotel guide you see a range of rates quoted for a particular location. The range could cover a lot of different variances that may exist at the location, but frequently it is used to indicate how much you'll be paying, depending on whether or not you go for things like "beachside view," microwave in the room, and so on. If you want to save a fair amount on the nightly rate, take the room that doesn't have these add-ons. In general, most of these amenities sound better than they really are because chances are you'll not be spending much time in the room when you're on vacation—so why pay for them?

Ask for the long-term rates if you are staying five consecutive nights.

Depending on the specific hotel establishment or chain, you may be eligible to receive special rates if you agree to stay there for a certain number of consecutive nights. The number is usually five or seven, but here again, I would try some negotiating. Five nights in the same hotel is a pretty substantial period of time to be checked in at one place. Depending on the quality of the hotel and on how many people you're traveling with, five nights can leave you with a bill in excess of $1,000. At that price, I would definitely make a play for lower rates on the basis of length of stay. Now, it's true that even three nights at some hotels can leave you with a very expensive bill, but because many people will stay for two or three nights—even four nights—you won't really have much leverage with which to bargain for a break.

Consider alternatives to standard hotels and motels.

If the truth be told, there are many different kinds of places you can go to stay for a night or a series of nights. Hotels and motels are two options, but there are lots of others. What's more, many of these alternatives exist with the budget-conscious in mind, so you may want to pay close attention to what is offered if you want to *really* save on your nightly stays.

One of the better options is the well-known hostel. A hostel is an inn where beds are provided, common areas like kitchens and bathrooms are provided, and you basically engage in "do-it-yourself" lodging—cooking your own meals, and so on. Hostels are real cheap stays; if you want to learn more, contact the American Youth Hostels at (202) 783-6161. There are a few different guidebooks available from the organization that provide information on hostel locations throughout the world. Unless you're a member, expect to pay around $10 for each publication.

You may be familiar with "bed and breakfasts," which are usually quaint hotels that offer meal packages with the overall price of the stay. Be forewarned, though, that not all bed and breakfasts are bargains. Some pride themselves on their exclusivity and charge rates that can even be in excess of well-known, upscale hotels. You will have to hunt among what is available to find the value you're seeking. My suggestion is to purchase any of the several bed-and-breakfast guides that are available at bookstores, most of which seem to be very comprehensive, so that you can make a more-informed decision. The Internet is a valuable tool for bed-and-breakfast information.

Finally, let's talk about going back to college . . . literally! You may not know this, but you can rent dorm rooms at many colleges and universities. In general, the nightly cost runs from about $15 to maybe as high as $35. Furthermore, you are allowed to use the campus facilities while you're a guest there. If you want to find out more about what's available, purchase the *Budget Lodging Guide* for around $16.95 (includes shipping and handling) by writing to Campus Travel Service, Box 5468, Fullerton, CA 92838. This resource also contains information on other low-cost alternatives, as well.

Car Rental

Renting a car has become essential to the vacations of so many. Unfortunately, it has also become quite complex, as well. Keep your eyes peeled for all of the costs and fine print on automobile rental contracts—specifically, the expenses you will be on the hook for. Sadly, too many in the car-rental business have chosen to forsake plain, fair dealing in favor of the opportunity to make a bundle in the form of a "quick hit." Here are some simple strategies that you can use to make your car renting experience a lot less expensive and a lot more pleasurable.

 Talk to your travel agent
before you rent a car.

Travel agents sometimes get a bad rap for adding to the cost of a vacation, rather than for bringing value. While it's true that travel agents need to be paid for their services, the cost of that compensation can be more than offset by the quality of the deals they can find. Travel agents have access to many different computer search and quote systems that help them find much better deals than you would be able to find on your own. This is as true in the area of car rental as it is in any other aspect of travel. So when you need to rent a car, contact your travel agent first and see how much money you can save.

 Avoid renting a car
at the airport.

In the world of car rental, it is the airport rental that generally makes the most money for the agencies. The chief reason rates are so high is because you are considered "captive," that is, you just landed in the airport, and now you need a set of wheels to go anywhere from there. Also there are usually exorbitant fees and special airport taxes that merchants located at airports must pay, so those costs need to be covered. Overall, then, if you choose to rent your car at the airport, you can expect to pay handsomely for the privilege.

A sharp alternative to renting at the airport is to rent off-site, which means at a location that is not even close to the airport. By doing this, you will not be stuck paying the artificially inflated rates that are usually found at airports; rather, you will be able to pay what the local market normally bears. The best way to handle this process is to take a taxi or shuttle to your hotel, and then once you've checked in look in the local Yellow Pages for car rental agencies.

 Rent your car from an agency that specializes in unglamorous vehicles.

This strategy is actually a continuation of the same thought that provoked the last strategy. You may have heard the names "Ugly Duckling" and "Rent-a-Wreck" used in conjunction with the car rental industry. These are two companies that specialize in renting very average-looking cars. They really aren't necessarily "ugly" or "wrecks"; they're just not top-of-the-line new-model cars. The fact is, these cars are very functional, and you'll be able to rent them for a lot less than you would pay for a "great deal" from Hertz or Avis. Now, I'm not saying that you'll necessarily want to choose this option if you plan on doing a great deal of driving, but if your driving will consist of doing what it takes to get around locally, then this choice should do just fine.

 Don't pick up the collision damage waiver from the rental agency.

Car rental agencies are sometimes fond of saying that they do not sell insurance; this is usually in rebuttal to the coverages you're asked to buy when you rent a vehicle. It's true that they don't sell "insurance," per se (if they did, they would have to submit to the jurisdiction of the state insurance commissioner), but they essentially *do* sell it in the form of "collision damage waivers" and "loss damage waivers." The agencies make these coverages sound wonderful, saying that if you buy them you will have no financial responsibility of any kind if the car is damaged. However, you should really consider skipping the offer and keeping the approximately $15 a day the coverages cost in your pocket. As long as you are already a car owner and have all of the necessary insurance coverages your state requires, you should be adequately covered. Also, if you're paying with a credit card, you may receive excellent coverage from that resource, as well.

Bottom line: Before going in to check out your car, make sure you know what your own insurance coverage, as well as your relevant credit card, will be able to do for you in this capacity.

Cruises

The cruise is considered by many to be the symbol of glamorous vacation living. So often you'll hear people say, "I want to take a cruise just one time before I die." I have taken several in my time, and I have enjoyed every one. There is nothing quite like taking a vacation on the open seas, especially these days when cruise ships are so artfully constructed that they manage to combine safety and comfort with what is sometimes unimaginable enjoyment.

Cruises, though, are vacations that normally do not come cheap. If you want to get a good deal on a cruise, you'll have to keep your eyes open and your wits about you. It *can* be done, but you'll have to follow the value-hunter's rules of the road or, in this case, rules of the sea.

 Remember the easiest way to get a bargain: book early.

Cruise lines are no different than any other business entity; the earlier they can land your money, the happier they'll be. To do that, many companies will grant you a substantial break on the standard rate in order to get your money in the bank more quickly. Make sure you call the cruise line to secure this "early bird" discount. Also, shop around. All early-booking deals are not alike. Spend some time getting a solid handle on where and when you want to go, then find several cruise lines that might fit your requirements. Shop your rates as early as possible. By doing this sort of head-start planning, there's no question that you'll be able to save big over the rates you'd pay if you were cruising in the near-term.

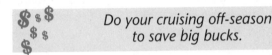

Do your cruising off-season to save big bucks.

It doesn't take a rocket scientist to figure out that cruises to the Caribbean are going to be more expensive during the winter months, and cruises to places like Alaska are going to be more expensive during the summer, so depending on where you want to cruise, try to schedule your vacation during the off-season for your location. While you wouldn't be able to cruise in Alaska during the dead of winter, it is possible to go early in the spring and late in the fall. If you're okay with that, and you've always wanted to cruise to Alaska, then you should be able to realize a nice discount. Same thing for the warmer climates. If you can take the heat, then cruising to an exotic tropical port in the summer may be just the ticket for you to save some money.

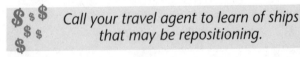

Call your travel agent to learn of ships that may be repositioning.

Repositioning is a cruise industry term used to describe a ship that is going out of service in one part of the world and going into service in another. When that happens, there can be great deals to be had. My suggestion is that you have a travel agent do your hunting for you.

*Assemble a group
to gain a group discount.*

If you've been thinking that it might be fun to go on vacation with several people, then a cruise might be just the way to do two things: take that long-anticipated group tour and save a bundle on cruise rates. As with just about anything, buying in bulk saves. If you can assemble a group of at least ten people, then it's going to be very likely that you all can enjoy a nice break on your ticket prices. Contact your travel agent or cruise lines of choice to find out what requirements have to be met for you to enjoy the pricing benefits that come with booking a large group.

*If you have a special skill or talent
you might be able to cruise for free.*

One of the biggest challenges for cruise lines is to keep the passengers happy. Even though the ships are big and cruising the open seas can be quite exciting, people are still people, which means that we're *all* prone to becoming victims to monotony. To remedy this, cruise lines try to come up with as many new and exciting things as they can find to keep passengers happy. If you have a special ability or talent, you might be able to cruise for free.

Now, don't think that the only kinds of skills or talents that will be attractive to cruise lines are fire-eaters or lounge singers. Cruises offer lectures, the teaching of games, and many other activities that require specialists of one sort or another. Plus, if you're going on a cruise geared to families, then there may be free-berth opportunities, or at least substantial discounts, available to teachers and day-care workers who don't mind doing some work while they're on board. To find out more, contact the personnel departments of the cruise lines you're considering.

If you're celebrating a personal milestone, tell the cruise line.

It is not uncommon to see discounts given to people who are celebrating personal milestones in their lives. Couples looking to cruise to celebrate a big wedding anniversary and newlyweds are but two examples of people who may be able to enjoy a discount off the standard fare. (You may have to trade some anonymity for your discount—like when you're made the center of attention at dinner—but there's nothing wrong with that . . . especially if it leaves more of your bank account intact.)

Book the lowest-cost cabin then try to upgrade.

If you're interested in cruising on a larger ship, then this strategy may work out well for you. Larger ships will usually have more space available at any given time, which means that the possibility of receiving an upgrade is greater. The best candidates to receive upgrades are usually the aforementioned anniversary and wedding celebrants, senior citizens, members of travel clubs, and frequent travelers—people who are either celebrating a special occasion or those who are "professional" travelers, who will be more likely to give repeat business to the line. Still, if you don't fit into one of these groups, don't feel that you can't ask with any degree of confidence that your request will be honored—you can.

*Always check on free airfare
to the departure city.*

Some cruises will advertise that there is free airfare to the departure city. This may be something extra or a perk that's wrapped into the cruise package. Either way, free airfare can represent a substantial enough savings to make the difference between an affordable cruise and one on which you'll have to pass.

11

Big Savings Online

If you are among the estimated 50 million Americans who use the Internet, you may already know that it is truly an unbelievable place to find bargains on everything from travel to real estate. If you are not a "computer head" and have not yet ventured into the cyberworld of the Internet, you will definitely have a change of heart after reading this chapter. Having access to the Internet is one of the most effective means to save money I have found. I am so excited about the Internet that I recently spent over six months building a website that boasts over one million direct and secondary links to the best and most profitable places to visit on the Internet. (To visit this site simply go to www.JLParis.com.)

The Internet can be a wonderful and truly amazing resource. The key is to remember to be just as careful (if not more) when doing business on the Internet as you would be if you were dealing in person with a company. Finding the right websites can be hard work, so be sure to keep good notes and addresses of your favorite sites so you can go back to them quickly. Also, it is a good idea to register your name in the guestbook of your favorite sites so that you can be alerted of any special offers or new additions to the site.

In this chapter, you will be introduced to the most wonderful source of bargains and deals you will ever find this side of your local flea market.

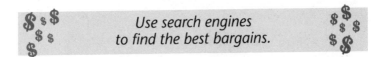

Use search engines to find the best bargains.

The most useful tool you will find on the Internet is called a "search engine." A search engine is kind of a cyber version of directory assistance—but better. For example, you usually can't call "information" and ask them to give you the name of a pizza delivery restaurant in your area; you must tell them the exact name of the business and sometimes the location. Search engines can produce information on just about any topic you are researching, regardless of the fact that you may not have any more to go on than a single word. You will be absolutely amazed when you discover how easy it is to use a search-engine service. For example, after getting online, click on the search button then enter "travel bargains." Literally thousands of web site destinations will be listed on the screen for you to browse and then, with a simple point and click of your mouse you will be at any web site you select.

I have found my searches to be most successful by using the major search engines. By sticking with the larger search services you can be relatively assured that most web sites with the information you need will be registered with them. Since there are almost 1000 search engines operating worldwide, it is unlikely that web builders will list themselves with each and every search service, especially those that are among the more obscure. Listed below are the ten search engines that I recommend:

Alta Vista: www.altavista.digital.com

Excite: www.excite.com

Galaxy: www.einet.net

HotBot: www.hotbot.com

Infoseek: www.infoseek.com

Lycos: www.lycos.com

Webcrawler: http://webcrawler.com

Wired Source: www.hotwired.com/cybrarian

WWW Virtual Library: www.infohiway.com

Yahoo!: www.yahoo.com

Without being overly technical, it is important for you to understand how search engine services work, so that you can perform your searches as quickly as possible. Most search engines operate on the honor system, allowing each website to submit about 25 words that become searchable by the service. These words or phrases are chosen entirely by the website creator and there is usually very little checking done by the search engine services to be sure that a given website is fairly or accurately representing their site.

I point this out to alert you that every search you perform will undoubtedly yield some web site listings that have nothing to do with your given topic. This is due to the web builders not doing a good job of providing a proper list of search phrases or is sometimes purposeful deception on the part of the website operators. One example is the word *Hawaii*. Internet statistics show that the word Hawaii is one of the seven most requested search words. Consequently, many individuals who have nothing about Hawaii on their site are submitting the word Hawaii as one of the descriptors of their site. You will see these kinds of tricks frequently on the Internet. All you can really do is quickly click out of their sites and go back to your original listing of other sites that met your criteria and continue on with the process.

*Be as detailed as possible
when submitting your searches.*

Many times the biggest challenge in utilizing the search services is taking the time to be specific about your search. For example, if you were in the market to purchase life insurance it would be too broad of a search to submit "insurance," a better choice would be "term life insurance." To save a tremendous amount of time you can go to www.JLParis.com. You will find links for virtually every financial topic imaginable. In the main menu of www.JLParis.com, click on ENTER and you will find the listing "$$$ Web Sites." By clicking on this button you will have access to my personal list of recommended sites. These sites are all "hotlinked," which means you can simply click on them and you will go directly to the site. You will be able to return to the www.JLParis.com site by using the "back" button on your browser.

Get free e-mail.

Microsoft offers free e-mail at www.hotmail.com. I personally utilize this service and find it is a great way to keep in touch with friends. I use this as my personal e-mail address to keep it separate from my business e-mail box, which is read by my employees as well as myself. To get your free e-mail box simply go to the website and follow the easy instructions. You will be set up in about five minutes.

*Beware of deals
that look too good to be true.*

The Internet is a ripe arena for scam artists. First of all, to start a business on the Internet, all you need is a few hundred dollars. This means that virtually anyone can get on the Internet and start selling their products or services without any background checks or office locations—with total anonymity. There is virtually no other venue that you can compare this to. For example, if you were to purchase an ad in your local newspaper, they would want to see a business license, review your advertisement to be sure it was a legitimate offer, make sure you gave an accurate address, and, if required, check to see that you possess the appropriate licenses.

*Follow basic common sense
guidelines you would follow if doing
business in person.*

If the offer sounds unbelievably good, check out the company. You can call the attorney general of the state where the company is based and ask if there is any record of complaints or problems. You can also check with the Better Business Bureau in the city where the business is located. Another kind of back-door checking is to put the company's name in your search engine and search the Internet for any listings made by individuals who have had a positive or negative experience with the company. In one case, I found literally dozens of negative newsgroup postings about a firm I was considering purchasing a business course from.

Recommended Websites

For your convenience, listed below are some of the main websites I recommend.

Auto Values

Autosite: www.autosite.com

AutoWeb Interactive: www.autoweb.com

Car Link: www.carlist.com

Edmund's Automotive Buyers Guide:
www.edmunds.com

Kelly Blue Book: www.kbb.com

Banks

Bank Rate Monitor: www.bankrate.com

Independent Bankers Association of America:
www.ibaa.org

My Bank Directory: www.mybank.com

Online and Worldwide Banking Directory:
www.orcc.com ("FI Directory")

U.S. Federal Deposit Insurance Corporation:
www.fdic.gov

College Financial Aid

CastPress: www.castpress.com

Federal Direct Loan Program: www.ed.gov/

Finaid: www.finaid.com

MOLIS (Minority On-Line Information) Scholarship
Search: www.fie.com/molis

Nellie Mae Loan Link: www.nelliemae.org

PNC Bank: Education Loan Center:
www.eduloans.pncbank.com

Sallie Mae Loan Link: www.salliemae.com

Your Best College for the Best Price:
www.pathfinder.com/money/colleges

Credit

BankCard Holders of America: www.dca.org

Best Picks: www.jlparis.com/creditnews.htm

ConsumerInfo.Com: www.consumerinfo.com

Credit Bureau Links:
www.yahoo.com/Business_and_Economy/Compa-
nies/Information/Investigative_Services/
Background_Verification/Credit_Report_Services/

The Credit Card Network: www.creditnet.com

Getsmart: www.getsmart.bfc.pilot.net

TIAC: 12 Credit Card Secrets Banks Don't Want You to
Know: www.consumer.com/consumer (online
brochure)

Free Stuff

Deals of the Day:
www.imall.com/stores/dotd/inc/dotd.shtml

The Free Forum: www.freeforum.com

A Great Way to Shop: www.greatway.com

Tabbie's Free-Stuff: www.freestuff.pair.com

Volition: www.volition.com/free.html

Insurance

AccuQuote: www.accuquote.com

Insurance News Network: www.insure.com/auto

Golden Rule Insurance Company: www.goldenrule.com

Jim Paris' Auto Insurance Strategies:
www.jlparis.com/autoins.htm

Jim Paris' Health Insurance Strategies:
www.jlparis.com/healthins.htm

Quicken's Insuremarket: www.insuremarket.com

Six Ways to Save on Homeowner's Insurance:
www.pathfinder.com/money/saveon/1996/
homeins.html

What You Should Know About Buying Life Insurance:
www.pueblo.gsa.gov/cic/AT-cicsearch.cgi

Internet Scams

Better Business Bureau: www.bbb.com

Consumer World: www.consumerworld.org

CyberCop Precinct House: www.ucan.org

Federal Trade Commission Consumer Brochures:
www.webcom/~lewrose/brochures.html

National Fraud Information Center: www.fraud.com

NetCheck: www.netcheck.com

WebWatchdog: www.webwatchdog.com

Investment

DLJdirect Inc.: www.dljdirect.com

Financenter: www.financenter.com

Invest-O-Rama: www.investorama.com

InvestorGuide: www.investorguide.com

James L. Paris Financial Services:
www.jlparis.com/jamesl.htm

Microsoft Investor:
   www.investor.msn.com/common/welcome.asp

Small Companies Links:
   www.SmallCapInvestor.com/sclinks.asp

Wall Street Research Net: www.wsrn.com

Legal Help

Attorney Find: www.attorneyfind.com

Attorney Finder: www.attyfind.com

LawInfo: www.lawinfo.com

Tax Help

H&R Block: www.hrblock.com

H&R Block's Refund Calculator: www.hrblock.com
   /tax/refund/

IRS: www.irs.ustreas.gov

Kiplinger TaxCut: www.conductor.com

Secure Tax: www.securetax.com

State Tax Information: www.loc.gov/global/state/
   stategov.html

Tax Wizard: www.taxwizard.com

Turbo Tax: www.intuit.com/turbotax/

Travel

1travel.com: www.1travel.com

11th Hour Vacations: www.11thhourvacations.com

Airline Webs: www. jlparis.com/airline.htm

American Express Travel:
   www.americanexpress.com/travel/index.html

Best Fares: www.bestfares.com

Budget Travel Webs: www. jlparis.com/budget.htm

Business Travel Webs: www. jlparis.com/business.htm

Cruise Webs: www. jlparis.com/cruise.htm

Discount Airfares and On-line Reservations: www.etn.nl/discount.htm

Expedia Travel Agent: www.expedia.msn.com/daily/home/default.hts

Flifo: www.flifo.com

Fodor's Travel Publications: www.fodors.com

Frommers: www.frommers.com

Genie Travel Services: www.genietravel.com

Internet Travel Network: www.itn.net

Lodging Webs: www. jlparis.com/lodging.htm

Newport Beach Travel: www.nbtravel.com

Preview Travel: www.previewtravel.com

Rental Cars Webs: www. jlparis.com/rental.htm

RV's & Parks Webs: www. jlparis.com/rvs-parks.htm

Sabre Web Reservations: www.webreservations.com

Sapphire Swan: www.sapphireswan.com/webguide/

Timeshare Webs: www. jlparis.com/timeshar.htm

Travel Agents: www.jlparis.com/travel1.htm

Travel Source: www.travelsource.com/index.html

Travelocity: www.travelocity.com

Travel Time: www.traveltime.com

Vacation Webs: www. jlparis.com/vacation.htm

Internet Service Providers

America Online: www.aol.com

The largest internet service provider, "AOL" offers 100 free hours of on-line time for the first month of usage. Service runs about $21* per month. It has several chat forums and child protection screening programs, but its browser does not give the sharp representation of colors and text presented by the more advanced websites.

AT&T: www.att.net

The long distance carrier AT&T joined in the game of internet service providing. For $19.95 per month they provide access and the choice of either Netscape or IE 3.0 browser capabilities. On-line viewing of websites is better than with AOL, but the speed of access is limited in most parts of the country to 28.8 kbps.

Compuserve: www.compuserve.com

Compuserve has over two million customers and is a subsidiary of AOL. It has many of the same features as AOL.

IDT: www.idt.net

At only $19.95 per month, IDT offers—

- software that gives you a full graphic connection with unlimited, uncensored access to the Internet. IRC and Telnet client software is also included.

- free Netscape (version 3.0), the number-one web browser on the market.

- e-mail capabilities with up to 2-megabytes of storage space.

---

* Please call the individual services to confirm program prices.

MSN.COM: www.msn.com/welcome

MSN, Microsoft's own internet service provider, provides free Internet Explorer 4.0 browser on disk with the MSN program. You must have Windows 95 to use MSN. Billing begins after your free trial is over.

MSN Premier Unlimited Plan: Unlimited use of MSN and the Internet at one simple price—$19.95 per month.

MSN Premier Plan: 5 hours of access per month to MSN and the Internet for $6.95 per month, with each additional charged at $2.50.

MSN Premier ISDN Flat Rate Plan: ISDN (Integrated Services Digital Network) access to great MSN content for one monthly charge—$49.95 per month. Single or Dual Channel ISDN.

Factory Outlet Malls

Following is a list of factory outlet malls located across the United States. This list is in no way intended to represent a complete roster of the outlet malls; the selections were based largely on the number and variety of stores available at each .location.

Alabama

Boaz Outlet Center
425 McClesky Street
Boaz, Alabama 35957

Riviera Centre Factory Stores
2601 South McKenzie Street
Foley, Alabama 36535

Arizona

Casa Grande Factory Stores
440 North Camino Mercado
Casa Grande, Arizona 85222

Tanger Factory Outlet Centers
2300 East Tanger Drive
Casa Grande, Arizona 85222

Arkansas

Hot Springs Factory Outlet Stores
4332 Central Avenue
Hot Springs, Arkansas 71913

California

American Tin Cannery Factory
  Outlets
125 Ocean View Boulevard
Pacific Grove, California 93950

Desert Hills Factory Stores
48650 Seminole Road
Cabazon, California 92230

Factory Merchants Barstow
2837 Lenwood Road
Barstow, California 92311

Lake Elsinore Outlet Center
17600 Collier Avenue
Lake Elsinore, California 92530

Folsom Premium Outlets
13000 Folsom Boulevard
Folsom, California 95630

Pacific West Outlet Center
8375-46 Arroyo Circle
Gilroy, California 95020

San Diego Factory Outlet Center
4498 Camino de la Plaza
San Ysidro, California 92173

The Factory Stores of America at
   Nut Tree
321-2 Nut Tree Road
Vacaville, California 95687

Colorado

Castle Rock Factory Shops
5050 Factory Shops Boulevard
Castle Rock, Colorado 80104

Silverthorne Factory Stores
145 Stephens Way
Silverthorne, Colorado 80498

Connecticut

Factory Outlets at Norwalk
11 Rowan Street
Norwalk, Connecticut 06855

Delaware

Ocean Outlets Factory Outlet
   Center
Route 1
Rehoboth Beach, Delaware 19971

Florida

Belz Factory Outlet World
5401 West Oakridge Road
Orlando, Florida 32819

Gulf Coast Factory Shops
5461 Factory Shops Boulevard
Ellenton, Florida 34222

Sawgrass Mills
12801 West Sunrise Boulevard
Sunrise, Florida 33323

St. Augustine Outlet Center
2700 State Road 16
St. Augustine, Florida 32092

Georgia

Lake Park Mill Store Plaza
5327 Mill Store Road
Lake Park, Georgia 31636

Tanger Factory Outlet Center
198 Tanger Drive
Commerce, Georgia 30529

Hawaii

Waikele Premium Outlets
H-1 Freeway and Kamehameha
   State Highway
Waipahu, Oahu
Hawaii

Idaho

Boise Factory Outlets
6852 Eisenman Road
Boise, Idaho 83705

Factory Outlets at Post Falls
West 4300 River Bend Avenue
Post Falls, Idaho 83854

Illinois

Gurnee Mills Mall
6170 West Grand Avenue
Gurnee, Illinois 60031

The Piano Factory Outlet Mall
410 South First Street
St. Charles, Illinois 60174

Indiana

Horizon Outlet Center—
  Edinburgh
11626 N.E. Executive Drive
Edinburgh, Indiana 46124

Horizon Outlet Center—Fremont
6245 North Old 27
Fremont, Indiana 46737

Lighthouse Place
601 Wabash
Michigan City, Indiana 46360

Iowa

Tanger Factory Outlet Center
Tanger Drive
Williamsburg, Iowa 52361

Kansas

Lawrence Riverfront Plaza Factory
  Outlets
One Riverfront Plaza
Lawrence, Kansas 66044

Whites Factory Outlet Center
Interstate 70 and Highway 25
Colby, Kansas 67701

Kentucky

Factory Stores of America
401 Commercial Drive
Georgetown, Kentucky 40324

West Kentucky Factory Outlets
208 Outlet Avenue
Eddyville, Kentucky 42038

Louisiana

Slidell Factory Outlet Center
1000 Caruso Boulevard
Slidell, Louisiana 70461

Tanger Factory Outlet Center
2200 Tanger Boulevard
Gonzales, Louisiana 70737

Maine

Freeport Outlets
U.S. Route 1
Freeport, Maine 04032

Tanger Factory Outlet Center 1
283 U.S. Route 1
Kittery, Maine 03904

The Maine Outlet
U.S. Route 1
Kittery, Maine 03904

Maryland

Chesapeake Village at Queenstown
441 Chesapeake Village Road
Queenstown, Maryland 21658

Perryville Outlet Center
68 Heather Lane
Perryville, Maryland 21903

Massachusetts

Cape Cod Factory Outlet Mall
1 Factory Outlet Road
Cape Cod (Sagamore),
  Massachusetts 02561

Howland Place Designer Outlet
  Center
651 Orchard Street
New Bedford, Massachusetts
  02744

Quality Factory Outlets
638 Quequechan Street
Fall River, Massachusetts 02721

Michigan

Horizon Outlet Center—Monroe
14500 LaPlaisance Road
Monroe, Michigan 48161

Outlets at Birch Run
12240 South Beyer Road
Birch Run, Michigan 48415

Outlets at Holland
12330 James Street
Holland, Michigan 49424

Minnesota

Horizon Outlet Center—
  Woodbury
10150 Hudson Road
Woodbury, Minnesota 55125

Pottery Place Outlet Center
2000 West Main Street
Red Wing, Minnesota 55066

Mississippi

Vicksburg Factory Outlets
4000 South Interstate 20 Frontage
  Road
Vicksburg, Mississippi 39180

Missouri

Belz Factory Outlet Mall
100 Mall Parkway
Wentzville, Missouri 63385

Factory Outlet Village Osage
  Beach
East Highway 54
Osage Beach, Missouri 65065

Montana

Whitefish Outlet Mall
Highway 93
Whitefish, Montana 59937

Nevada

Belz Factory Outlet World
7400 Las Vegas Boulevard South
Las Vegas, Nevada 89123

Factory Stores of America at Las
  Vegas
9155 Las Vegas Boulevard
Las Vegas, Nevada 89123

New Hampshire

North Hampton Factory Outlet
  Center
Route 1, Lafayette Road
North Hampton, New Hampshire
  03862

Settlers' Green Outlet Village Plus
Route 16
North Conway, New Hampshire
  03860

New Jersey

Harmon Cove Outlet Center
20 Enterprise Avenue
Secaucus, New Jersey 07094

Liberty Village Factory Outlets
One Church Street
Flemington, New Jersey 08822

New Mexico

Santa Fe Factory Stores
8380 Cerrillios Road
Santa Fe, New Mexico 87505

New York

Apollo Plaza Manufacturer's Outlet
   Center
Route 17 West, Exit 106
Monticello, New York 12701

Factory Outlet Mall
1900 Military Road
Niagara Falls, New York 14304

Woodbury Common Factory
   Outlets
Route 32
Central Valley, New York 10917

North Carolina

Burlington Manufacturers Outlet
   Center
2389 Corporation Parkway
Burlington, North Carolina 27215

Factory Stores of America Outlet
   Center
1209 Industrial Park Drive
Smithfield, North Carolina 27577

Ohio

Jeffersonville Outlet Center
1100 McArthur Road
Jeffersonville, Ohio 43128

Ohio Factory Shops
8000 Factory Shops Boulevard
Jeffersonville, Ohio 43128

Oklahoma

Tanger Factory Outlet Center
200 Tanger Drive
Stroud, Oklahoma 74079

Oregon

The Factory Outlets at
   Lincoln City
Highway 101 and East Devils
   Lake Road
Lincoln City, Oregon 97367

Pennsylvania

Factory Stores of America
801 Hill Avenue
Wyomissing, Pennsylvania 19610

Franklin Mills
1455 Franklin Mills Circle
Philadelphia, Pennsylvania 19114

Manufacturers Outlet Mall
Pennsylvania Turnpike, Exit 22
Morgantown, Pennsylvania 19543

Rockvale Square Factory Outlet
   Village
35 South Willowdale Drive
Lancaster, Pennsylvania 17602

South Carolina

Hilton Head Factory Stores
1024 Highway 278, Box B-5
Bluffton, South Carolina 29910

Outlet Park at Waccama
3200 Pottery Drive
Myrtle Beach, South Carolina
   29577

Tennessee

Belz Factory Outlet Mall
3536 Canada Road
Lakeland, Tennessee 38002

Belz Factory Outlet Mall
2655 Teaster Lane
Pigeon Forge, Tennessee 37853

Factory Stores of America
Outlet Center Drive
Nashville, Tennessee 37219

Texas

Conroe Outlet Center
1111 League Line Road
Conroe, Texas 77303

Gainesville Factory Shops
4321 North Interstate Highway 35
Gainesville, Texas 76240

San Marcos Factory Shops
3939 Interstate Highway 35 South
San Marcos, Texas 78666

Southwest Outlet Center
104 Interstate Highway 35 N.E.
Hillsboro, Texas 76645

Utah

Factory Stores at Park City
6699 North Landmark Drive
Park City, Utah 84060

Factory Stores of America
12101 South Factory Outlet Drive
Draper, Utah 84020

Virginia

Potomac Mills
2700 Potomac Mills Circle
Prince William, Virginia 22192

The Williamsburg Outlet Mall
6401 Richmond Road
Lightfoot, Virginia 23090

Washington

Centralia Factory Outlet Center
201 South Pearl
Centralia, Washington 98531

Pacific Edge Outlet Center
448 Fashion Way
Burlington, Washington 98233

West Virginia

Blue Ridge Outlet Center
400 West Stephen Street
Martinsburg, West Virginia 25401

Wisconsin

Factory Outlet Centre
7700 120 Avenue
Kenosha, Wisconsin 53142

Horizon Outlet Center—Oshkosh
3001 South Washburn
Oshkosh, Wisconsin 54904

Lakeside Marketplace
11211 120th Avenue
Kenosha, Wisconsin 53142

Appendix B

No Commission, Direct-Purchase Stocks

This is a list of stocks you can buy directly from the company without having to go through a broker. This is not a complete list of all no-commission, direct-purchase stocks, but these companies make initial purchases available to residents in at least 47 states. You will want to contact the company directly at the given phone number(s) if you desire additional information.

ABT Building Products Corp.
One Neenah Center, Suite 600
Neenah, WI 54956-3070
(414) 751-8611; (800) 774-4117
NASDAQ: ABTC

Advanta Corp.
Welsh and McKean Rds.
Spring House, PA 19477
(215) 444-5335; (800) 774-4117
NASDAQ: ADVNB

Aegon N.V.
c/o Morgan Guaranty Trust Co.
PO Box 9073
Boston, MA 02205
(800) 749-1687; (800) 774-4117
NYSE: AEG

AFLAC, Inc.
1932 Wynnton Rd.
Columbus, GA 31999
(800) 227-4756; (706) 323-3431
NYSE: AFL

AirTouch Communications, Inc.
One California St.
San Francisco, CA 94111
(415) 658-2000; (800) 233-5601

NYSE: ATI

American Recreation Centers, Inc.
11171 Sun Center Dr., Suite 120
Rancho Cordova, CA 95670
(916) 852-8005; (800) 522-6645

NASDAQ: AMRC

Ameritech Corp.
30 S. Wacker Dr.
Chicago, IL 60606
(888) 752-6248; (312) 750-5353;
(800) 774-4117

NYSE: AIT

Amoco Corp.
200 E. Randolph Dr.
Chicago, IL 60601
(800) 821-8100; (800) 446-2617;
(800) 774-4117

NYSE: AN

Amway Japan Ltd.
c/o Morgan Guaranty Trust Co.
PO Box 9073
Boston, MA 02205
(800) 749-1687; (800) 774-4117

NYSE: AJL

Arrow Financial Corp.
250 Glen St.
PO Box 307
Glens Falls, NY 12801
(518) 793-4121; (718) 921-8200

NASDAQ: AROW

Atlantic Energy, Inc.
6801 Black Horse Pike
PO Box 1334
Pleasantville, NJ 08232

(609) 645-4506

NYSE: ATE

Atmos Energy Corp.
PO Box 650205
Dallas, TX 75265-0205
(800) 382-8667; (800) 543-3038;
(800) 774-4117

NYSE: ATO

Banco Santander, S.A.
c/o Morgan Guaranty Trust Co.
PO Box 9073
Boston, MA 02205
(800) 749-1687; (800) 774-4117

NYSE: STD

Bard (C.R.), Inc.
730 Central Ave.
Murray Hill, NJ 07974
(908) 277-8000; (800) 828-1639;
(800) 446-2617

NYSE: BCR

Barnett Banks, Inc.
Shareholder Services Dept.
PO Box 40789
Jacksonville, FL 32203-0789
(904) 791-7668; (800) 328-5822

NYSE: BBI

BRE Properties, Inc.
One Montgomery St.,
    Telesis Tower, Suite 2500
San Francisco, CA 94104-5525
(415) 445-6530; (800) 368-8392;
(800) 774-4117

NYSE: BRE

British Airways PLC
c/o Morgan Guaranty Trust Co.
PO Box 9073
Boston, MA 02205
(800) 749-1687; (800) 774-4117

NYSE: BAB

British Telecommunications PLC
c/o Morgan Guaranty Trust Co.
PO Box 9073
Boston, MA 02205
(800) 749-1687; (800) 774-4117

NYSE: BTY

Cadbury Schweppes PLC
c/o Morgan Guaranty Trust Co.
PO Box 9073
Boston, MA 02205
(800) 749-1687; (800) 774-4117

NYSE: CSG

Capstead Mortgage Corp.
2711 N. Haskell Ave., Ste. 900
Dallas, TX 75204
(214) 874-2323; (800) 527-7844

NYSE: CMO

Carpenter Technology Corp.
101 West Bern St.
Reading, PA 19612-4662
(610) 208-2000; (800) 822-9828;
(800) 446-2617

NYSE: CRS

Central & South West Corp.
PO Box 660164
Dallas, TX 75266-0164
(800) 527-5797; (800) 774-4117

NYSE: CSR

CMS Energy Corp.
Investor Services Dept.
212 W. Michigan Ave.
Jackson, MI 49201
(517) 788-1868; (800) 774-4117

NYSE: CMS

COMSAT Corp.
6560 Rock Spring Dr.
Bethesda, MD 20817

(301) 214-3200; (800) 524-4458

NYSE: CQ

Conrail, Inc.
Two Commerce Square
Philadelphia, PA 19101
(215) 209-4000; (800) 243-7812

NYSE: CRR

Crown American Realty Trust
Pasquerilla Plaza
Johnstown, PA 15907
(814) 536-4441; (800) 278-4353;
(800) 774-4117

NYSE: CWN

CSR Limited
c/o Morgan Guaranty Trust Co.
PO Box 9073
Boston, MA 02205
(800) 749-1687; (800) 774-4117

NASDAQ: CSRLY

Dassault Systemes S.A.
c/o Morgan Guaranty Trust Co.
PO Box 9073
Boston, MA 02205
(800) 749-1687; (800) 774-4117

NASDAQ: DASTY

Dean Witter, Discover & Co.
Two World Trade Center, 56
    Floor
New York, NY 10048
(800) 622-2393; (800) 228-0829

NYSE: DWD

Dominion Resources, Inc.
PO Box 26532
Richmond, VA 23261
(800) 552-4034

NYSE: D

DQE
PO Box 68

Pittsburgh, PA 15230-0068
(800) 247-0400; (412) 393-6167

NYSE: DQE

DTE Energy Co.
PO Box 33380
Detroit, MI 48232
(800) 551-5009; (800) 774-4117

NYSE: DTE

Duke Realty Investments, Inc.
8888 Keystone Crossing, Ste. 1200
Indianapolis, IN 46240
(800) 278-4353; (800) 774-4117;
(317) 574-3531

NYSE: DRE

Eastern Company
112 Bridge St.
Naugatuck, CT 06770
(203) 729-2255; (800) 633-3455

ASE: EML

Empresa Nacional de Electricidad
   S.A.
c/o Morgan Guaranty Trust Co.
PO Box 9073
Boston, MA 02205
(800) 749-1687; (800) 774-4117

NYSE: ELE

Energen Corp.
2101 Sixth Ave. N.
Birmingham, AL 35203
(800) 286-9178; (800) 774-4117

NYSE: EGN

Enova Corp.
101 Ash St.
San Diego, CA 92101

(619) 696-2020; (800) 821-2550;
(800) 307-7343

NYSE: ENA

Enron Corp.
1400 Smith St.
Houston, TX 77002
(713) 853-6161; (800) 446-2617;
(800) 662-7662

NYSE: ENE

Entergy Corp.
PO Box 61000
New Orleans, LA 70161
(504) 576-4218; (800) 333-4368;
(800) 225-1721

NYSE: ETR

Equitable Companies
787 Seventh Ave.
New York, NY 10019
(800) 437-8736; (800) 774-4117

NYSE: EQ

Exxon Corp.
PO Box 160369
Irving, TX 75016-0369
(800) 252-1800; (214) 444-1000

NYSE: XON

Fiat S.P.A.
c/o Morgan Guaranty Trust Co.
PO Box 9073
Boston, MA 02205
(800) 749-1687; (800) 774-4117

NYSE: FIA

First Commercial Corp.
400 W. Capitol Ave.
Little Rock, AR 72201
(501) 371-7000; (501) 371-6716;
(800) 482-8410

NASDAQ: FCLR

First USA, Inc.
1601 Elm St.
Dallas, TX 75201
(214) 849-2000; (800) 524-4458

NYSE: FUS

General Growth Properties, Inc.
55 W. Monroe, Suite 3100
Chicago, IL 60603-5060
(312) 551-5000; (888) 291-3713;
(800) 774-4117

NYSE: GGP

Grand Metropolitan PLC
c/o Morgan Guaranty Trust Co.
PO Box 9073
Boston, MA 02205
(800) 749-1687; (800) 774-4117

NYSE: GRM

Guidant Corp.
111 Monument Circle, 29 Floor
Indianapolis, IN 46204
(800) 537-1677; (800) 317-4445

NYSE: GDT

Hawaiian Electric Industries, Inc.
PO Box 730
Honolulu, HI 96808-0730
(808) 543-5662; (808) 532-5841

NYSE: HE

Hillenbrand Industries, Inc.
700 State Route 46 East
Batesville, IN 47006
(800) 286-9178; (800) 774-4117;
(800) 445-4802

NYSE: HB

Home Depot, Inc.
2727 Paces Ferry Road
Atlanta, GA 30339

(800) 730-4001; (800) 774-4117;
(770) 433-8211

NYSE: HD

Home Properties of NY, Inc.
850 Clinton Square
Rochester, NY 14604
(716) 546-4900; (800) 774-4117;
(800) 278-4353

NYSE: HME

Houston Industries, Inc.
Investor Services Dept.
PO Box 4505
Houston, TX 77210
(713) 629-3000; (800) 231-6406;
(800) 774-4117

NYSE: HOU

Illinova Corp.
Attn: Shareholder Services
500 S. 27 St.
Decatur, IL 62525-1805
(800) 800-8220; (800) 750-7011

NYSE: ILN

Imperial Chemical Industries PLC
c/o Morgan Guaranty Trust Co.
PO Box 9073
Boston, MA 02205
(800) 749-1687; (800) 774-4117

NYSE: ICI

Integon Corp.
PO Box 3199
Winston-Salem, NC 27102-3199
(910) 770-2000; (800) 826-3978;
(800) 446-2617

NYSE: IN

Interchange Financial Services
    Corp.
Park 80 West/Plaza Two
Saddle Brook, NJ 07662

240   No Commission, Direct-Purchase Stocks

(201) 703-2265; (212) 509-4000
ASE: ISB

Investors Financial Services Corp.
89 South St.
Boston, MA 02111
(617) 330-6700; (888) 333-5336
NASDAQ: IFIN

IPLCO Enterprises, Inc.
Shareholder Services
PO Box 798
Indianapolis, IN 46206-0798
(317) 261-8394; (888) 847-2526;
(800) 774-4117
NYSE: IPL

Johnson Controls, Inc.
Shareholder Services
PO Box 591
Milwaukee, WI 53201-0591
(414) 228-2363; (800) 828-1489
NYSE: JCI

Kellwood Co.
600 Kellwood Parkway
Chesterfield, MO 63017
(314) 576-3100; (800) 321-1355
NYSE: KWD

Kerr-McGee Corp.
PO Box 25861
Oklahoma City, OK 73125
(405) 270-3582 ; (800) 786-2556;
(800) 395-2662
NYSE: KMG

Lucent Technologies, Inc.
600 Mountain Ave.
Murray Hill, NJ 07974
(888) 582-3686; (908) 582-8500
NYSE: LU

Madison Gas & Electric Co.
133 S. Blair St.
PO Box 1231
Madison, WI 53701-1231
(608) 252-7000; (800) 356-6423
NASDAQ: MDSN

Mattel, Inc.
333 Continental Blvd.
El Segundo, CA 90245-5012
(888) 909-9922; (310) 252-2000
NYSE: MAT

McDonald's Corp.
McDonald's Plaza
Oak Brook, IL 60521
(630) 623-7428; (800) 228-9623;
(800) 774-4117
NYSE: MCD

MidAmerican Energy Co.
666 Grand Ave.
PO Box 9244
Des Moines, IA 50306-9244
(515) 242-4310; (800) 247-5211
NYSE: MEC

Minnesota Power & Light Co.
30 W. Superior St.
Duluth, MN 55802-2093
(218) 722-2641; (800) 535-3056;
(800) 774-4117
NYSE: MPL

Mobil Corp.
3225 Gallows Rd.
Fairfax, VA 22037-0001
(800) 648-9291; (703) 849-3000
NYSE: MOB

Morton International, Inc.
100 N. Riverside Plaza
Chicago, IL 60606-1596

(800) 990-1010; (800) 774-4117;
(800) 446-2617

NYSE: MII

National Westminster Bank PLC
c/o Morgan Guaranty Trust Co.
PO Box 9073
Boston, MA 02205
(800) 749-1687; (800) 774-4117

NYSE: NW

Nippon Telegraph and Telephone
   Corp.
c/o Morgan Guaranty Trust Co.
PO Box 9073
Boston, MA 02205
(800) 749-1687; (800) 774-4117

NYSE: NTT

NorAm Energy Corp.
1600 Smith St.
PO Box 2628
Houston, TX 77002
(800) 843-3445; (713) 654-7502;
(800) 316-6726

NYSE: NAE

Norsk Hydro A.S.
c/o Morgan Guaranty Trust Co.
PO Box 9073
Boston, MA 02205
(800) 749-1687; (800) 774-4117

NYSE: NHY

Norwest Corp.
Norwest Center
Sixth and Marquette
Minneapolis, MN 55479
(612) 667-1234; (888) 291-3713;
(800) 813-3324

NYSE: NOB

Novo-Nordisk A/S
c/o Morgan Guaranty Trust Co.

PO Box 9073
Boston, MA 02205
(800) 749-1687; (800) 774-4117

NYSE: NVO

Oneok, Inc.
PO Box 871
Tulsa, OK 74102-0871
(918) 588-7000; (800) 395-2662

NYSE: OKE

Owens Corning
1 Owens Corning Parkway
Toledo, OH 43659
(419) 248-8000; (800) 472-2210;
(800) 438-7465

NYSE: OWC

Pacific Dunlop Limited
c/o Morgan Guaranty Trust Co.
PO Box 9073
Boston, MA 02205
(800) 749-1687; (800) 774-4117

NASDAQ: PDLPY

Peoples Energy Corp.
Shareholder Services
PO Box 2000
Chicago, IL 60609-2000
(800) 901-8878; (800) 774-4117

NYSE: PGL

Pharmacia & Upjohn, Inc.
c/o Harris Trust and Savings Bank
PO Box A3309
Chicago, IL 60690
(800) 323-1849; (800) 286-9178;
(800) 774-4117

NYSE: PNU

Philadelphia Suburban Corp.
762 Lancaster Ave.
Bryn Mawr, PA 19010-3489

(610) 645-1013; (800) 205-8314;
(800) 774-4117

NYSE: PSC

Piedmont Natural Gas Co.
PO Box 33068
Charlotte, NC 28233
(800) 438-8410; (800) 633-4236;
(800) 774-4117

NYSE: PNY

Pinnacle West Capital Corp.
PO Box 52133
Phoenix, AZ 85072-2133
(800) 457-2983; (800) 774-4117

NYSE: PNW

Portland General Corp.
121 SW Salmon St.
Portland, OR 97204
(503) 464-8599; (800) 446-2617

NYSE: PGN

Procter & Gamble Co.
PO Box 5572
Cincinnati, OH 45201-5572
(800) 742-6253; (800) 764-7483

NYSE: PG

Public Service of New Mexico
PO Box 1047
Albuquerque, NM 87103-9937
(800) 545-4425

NYSE: PNM

Rank Group PLC
c/o Morgan Guaranty Trust Co.
PO Box 9073
Boston, MA 02205
(800) 749-1687; (800) 774-4117

NASDAQ: RANKY

Reader's Digest Association, Inc.
Pleasantville, NY 10570

(914) 238-1000; (800) 230-2771;
(800) 242-4653

NYSE: RDA

Regions Financial Corp.
417 N. 20 St.
Birmingham, AL 35203
(800) 922-3468; (800) 446-2617

NASDAQ: RGBK

Reuters Holdings PLC
c/o Morgan Guaranty Trust Co.
PO Box 9073
Boston, MA 02205
(800) 749-1687; (800) 774-4117

NASDAQ: RTRSY

SCANA Corp.
Shareholder Services 054
Columbia, SC 29218
(803) 733-6817; (800) 763-5891;
(800) 774-4117

NYSE: SCG

Sears, Roebuck & Co.
3333 Beverly Rd.
Hoffman Estates, IL 60179
(847) 286-2500; (888) 732-7788

NYSE: S

Sierra Pacific Resources
Shareholder Relations
PO Box 30150
Reno, NV 89520-3150
(702) 689-3610; (800) 662-7575

NYSE: SRP

Southern Union Company
Investor Relations
504 Lavaca, Suite 800
Austin, TX 78701
(512) 370-8302; (800) 793-8938;
(800) 736-3001

NYSE: SUG

TDK Corp.
c/o Morgan Guaranty Trust Co.
PO Box 9073
Boston, MA 02205
(800) 749-1687; (800) 774-4117

NYSE: TDK

Telefonos de Mexico S.A. de C.V.
    Series L
c/o Morgan Guaranty Trust Co.
PO Box 9073
Boston, MA 02205
(800) 749-1687; (800) 774-4117

NYSE: TMX

Tenneco, Inc.
127 King St.
Greenwich, CT 06831
(203) 863-1000; (800) 446-2617

NYSE: TEN

Texaco, Inc.
Investor Services Plan
2000 Westchester Ave.
White Plains, NY 10650
(800) 283-9785; (800) 774-4117

NYSE: TX

Tyson Foods, Inc.
2210 W. Oaklawn Dr.
Springdale, AR 72764
(800) 446-2617; (800) 822-7096;
(800) 317-4445

NASDAQ: TYSNA

Unilever NV
c/o Morgan Guaranty Trust Co.
PO Box 9073
Boston, MA 02205
(800) 749-1687; (800) 774-4117

NYSE: UN

Urban Shopping Centers, Inc.
900 N. Michigan Ave.

Chicago, IL 60611
(312) 915-2000; (800) 992-4566;
(800) 774-4117

NYSE: URB

U S West Communications Group
7800 E. Orchard Rd.
Englewood, CO 80111
(800) 537-0222; (303) 793-6500

NYSE: USW

U S West Media Group
7800 E. Orchard Rd.
Englewood, CO 80111
(303) 793-6500; (800) 537-0222

NYSE: UMG

UtiliCorp United, Inc.
Shareholder Relations
911 Main, Suite 3000
Kansas City, MO 64105
(816) 421-6600; (800) 487-6661;
(800) 884-5426

NYSE: UCU

Viad Corp.
Dial Tower
Phoenix, AZ 85077
(800) 453-2235; (602) 207-2010

NYSE: VVI

Wal-Mart Stores, Inc.
702 Southwest 8th St.
PO Box 116
Bentonville, AR 72716
(501) 273-4000; (800) 438-6278

NYSE: WMT

Western Resources, Inc.
PO Box 750320
Topeka, KS 66675-0320
(800) 527-2495; (800) 774-4117

NYSE: WR

Whitman Corp.
3501 Algonquin Rd.
Rolling Meadows, IL 60008
(847) 818-5000; (800) 660-4187;
(800) 446-2617

NYSE: WH

Wisconsin Energy Corp.
231 W. Michigan St.
PO Box 2949
Milwaukee, WI 53201
(414) 221-2345; (800) 558-9663

NYSE: WEC

WPS Resources Corp.
700 N. Adams St.
PO Box 19001
Green Bay, WI 54307
(414) 433-1050; (800) 236-1551

NYSE: WPS

York International Corp.
631 S. Richland Ave.
York, PA 17403
(717) 771-7890
(800) 437-6726; (800) 774-4117

NYSE: YRK

No-Load
Mutual Funds

$50 per Month

The following four mutual fund companies ("families"), will waive their initial lump-sum minimum investment requirements if you agree to enroll in their respective automatic investment programs. The families on this list ask that you agree to send at least $50 per month.

Founders Funds
2930 East Third Avenue
Denver, CO 80206
(303) 394-4404; (800) 525-2440; (303) 394-4021 (Fax)

Minimum Initial Lump-Sum Purchase: non-IRA—$1,000; IRA—$500
Automatic Investment Plan: minimum $50 per month

Invesco Funds
7800 E. Union Avenue, Suite 800
Denver, CO 80237
(303) 930-6300; (800) 525-8085

Minimum Initial Lump-Sum Purchase: non-IRA—$1000; IRA—$250
Automatic Investment Plan: minimum $50 per month

American Century Funds
4500 Main Street
P.O. Box 419200
Kansas City, MO 64141-6200
(816) 531-5575; (800) 345-2021

> *Minimum Initial Lump-Sum Purchase:* non-IRA—$2,500; IRA-no
> minimum
> *Automatic Investment Plan:* minimum $50 per month

T. Rowe Price Funds
100 E. Pratt Street
Baltimore, MD 21202
(410) 547-2308; (800) 638-5660

> *Minimum Initial Lump-Sum Purchase:* non-IRA—$2,500; IRA—
> $1,000
> *Automatic Investment Plan:* minimum $50 per month

$100 per Month

The following two mutual fund families will waive their initial lump-sum minimums if you agree to participate in their respective automatic investment plans to the tune of at least $100 per month.

Babson Funds
Three Crown Center
2440 Pershing Road
Kansas City, MO 64108
(816) 751-5900; (800) 422-2766; (816) 471-7826 (Fax)

> *Minimum Initial Lump-Sum Purchase:* non-IRA—$500 to $2,500
> depending on the individual fund; IRA —$250
> *Automatic Investment Plan:* minimum $100 per month

Gabelli Funds
One Corporate Center
Rye, NY 10580
(914) 921-5100; (800) 422-3554; (914) 921-5118 (Fax)

> *Minimum Initial Lump-Sum Purchase:* non-IRA—$1,000; IRA—
> $1,000
> *Automatic Investment Plan:* minimum $100 per month

Initial Lump-Sum Investments
of Less Than $1,000

The following two mutual fund families will let you make
minimum initial lump-sum purchases of their funds for less
than $1,000.

AARP Funds
160 Federal Street
Boston, MA 02110
(617) 439-4640; (800) 253-2277; (800) 821-6234 (Fax)

Minimum Initial Lump-Sum Purchase: non-IRA—$500; IRA—$250

Dupree Funds
P.O. Box 1149
Lexington, KY 40589
(606) 254-7741; (800) 866-0614; (606) 254-1399 (Fax)

Minimum Initial Lump-Sum Purchase: non-IRA—$100; IRA—$100

BIBLIOGRAPHY

The College Board. *College Costs and Financial Aid*. New York: College Entrance Examination Board, 1997.

Elliston, Bob. *What Car Dealers Won't Tell You*. New York: Penguin Books USA, Inc., 1996.

Goodman, Jordan E. *Everyone's Money Book*. Chicago: Dearborn Financial Publishing, Inc., 1998.

Jensen, Jamie. *Road Trip USA*. Chico, CA: Moon Publications, Inc., 1996.

Kiplinger's Buying and Selling a Home. Washington: Kiplinger Times Business, 1996.

Paris, James L. *Money Management for Those Who Don't Have Any*. Eugene, OR: Harvest House Publishers, 1997.

Do-It-Yourself Health. Time-Life Books. Alexandria: Time Life Inc., 1997.

More Sound Financial Advice

MONEY MANGEMENT FOR THOSE
WHO DON'T HAVE ANY
by James L. Paris

This easy-to-use handbook is the consummate, non-nonsense guide to achieving financial success in your life at little or no cost! Whether you are truly flat broke or just feel you are, *Money Mangement for Those Who Don't Have Any* is the key to helping you attain your life-long goals and dreams.

MORE FOR YOUR MONEY
by James L. Paris

This newly revised and expanded combination of the popular *Living Financially Free* and *Living Financially Free Workbook* is bursting with everything you need to manage your money. *More for Your Money* is packed with realistic strategies, simple, straightforward budget worksheets, and step-by-step instructions that anyone can understand and put into practice to ensure their financial future.

THE 15-MINUTE MONEY MANAGER
by Bob and Emilie Barnes

Learn how to manage your money without a business degree. Bob and Emilie Barnes show you how to save money on everything from groceries to clothing, utilities to taxes.

Dear Reader:

We would appreciate hearing from you regarding this Harvest House book. It will enable us to continue to give you the best in Christian publishing.

1. What most influenced you to purchase *Absolutely Amazing Ways to Save Money on Everything*?

☐ Author   ☐ Recommendations
☐ Subject matter ☐ Cover/Title
☐ Back cover copy ☐ Other

2. Where did you purchase this book?

☐ Christian bookstore ☐ Grocery store
☐ General bookstore   ☐ Other
☐ Department store

3. Your overall rating of this book:

☐ Excellent   ☐ Very good   ☐ Good   ☐ Fair   q Poor

4. How likely would you be to purchase other books by this author?

☐ Very likely   ☐ Somewhat likely   ☐ Not very likely   ☐ Not at all

5. What types of books most interest you? (Check all that apply.)

☐ Women's Books   ☐ Fiction
☐ Marriage Books   ☐ Biographies
☐ Current Issues   ☐ Children's Books
☐ Christian Living ☐ Youth Books
☐ Bible Studies   ☐ Other

6. Please check the box next to your age group.

☐ Under 18   ☐ 18-24   ☐ 25-34   ☐ 35-44   ☐ 45-54   ☐ 55 and over

Mail to:

Editorial Director
Harvest House Publishers
1075 Arrowsmith
Eugene, OR 97402

Name_____

Address_____

State _____   Zip _____

Thank you for helping us help you in future publications!